# THE EPISTLE TO THE EPHESIANS

# THE EPISTLE TO THE EPHESIANS

KARL BARTH

EDITED BY R. DAVID NELSON

TRANSLATED BY ROSS M. WRIGHT

B

Baker Academic

a division of Baker Publishing Group

Grand Rapids, Michigan

English edition © 2017 by Baker Publishing Group

Originally published in German as Karl Barth, «*Erklärung des Epheserbriefes W.S. 1921/22*», *Erklärungen des Epheser- und des Jakobusbriefes, 1919–1929*, hg. Jörg-Michael Bohnet, *Karl Barth Gesamtausgabe* 46.

German edition © 2009 by Theologischer Verlag Zürich

Published by Baker Academic
a division of Baker Publishing Group
PO Box 6287, Grand Rapids, MI 49516-6287
www.bakeracademic.com

Printed in the United States of America

All rights reserved. No part of this publication may be reproduced, stored in a retrieval system, or transmitted in any form or by any means—for example, electronic, photocopy, recording—without the prior written permission of the publisher. The only exception is brief quotations in printed reviews.

Library of Congress Cataloging-in-Publication Data
Names: Barth, Karl, 1886–1968, author.
Title: The Epistle to the Ephesians / Karl Barth ; edited by R. David Nelson ; translated by Ross M. Wright.
Description: Grand Rapid : Baker Academic, 2017. | Includes bibliographical references and index.
Identifiers: LCCN 2016047869 | ISBN 9780801030918 (cloth)
Subjects: LCSH: Bible. Ephesians—Criticism, interpretation, etc.
Classification: LCC BS2695.52 .B3713 2017 | DDC 227/.506—dc23
LC record available at https://lccn.loc.gov/2016047869

17 18 19 20 21 22 23 7 6 5 4 3 2 1

In keeping with biblical principles of creation stewardship, Baker Publishing Group advocates the responsible use of our natural resources. As a member of the Green Press Initiative, our company uses recycled paper when possible. The text paper of this book is composed in part of post-consumer waste.

# Contents

# Editor's Introduction

R. David Nelson

Karl Barth's lectures on Ephesians from 1921–22 are published for the first time in English in this little volume. The lectures provide a window into Barth's developing theology during the critical period of the early 1920s and right around the publication of the second edition of *Der Römerbrief* (1922).[1] Barth's interest in exegetical work in the New Testament emerged in the preceding decade in the context of his pastoral duties in the Swiss village of Safenwil. It was in Safenwil that Barth's study of Paul's Epistle to the Romans led to his well-known commentary, appearing in two very different published editions.[2] There he also preached serially through several other New Testament texts—including Acts, the Epistles to the Corinthians, Ephesians, Colossians, and the Epistle to the Hebrews—and taught through various portions of the Bible in study groups and confirmation classes.[3] Soon after his appointment to a professorship in Reformed theology at the University of Göttingen in 1921, he took on a lecture load that had him teaching exegesis through focused series on New Testament texts; offerings in theology and doctrine on topics such as Calvin, Zwingli, the theology of the Reformed confessions, and Schleiermacher;[4] and beginning in 1924 a cycle in

Christian dogmatics.[5] In addition to Ephesians, Barth lectured during the Göttingen period on James, 1 Corinthians 15, 1 John, Philippians, Colossians, and the Sermon on the Mount.[6] The Ephesians lectures came right at the beginning, composing—with a series on the Heidelberg Catechism—Barth's first lecture load, which he delivered during the *Wintersemester* of 1921/22.[7]

Barth's lectures are interesting not only for the glimpse they offer into this early and critical stage of his theological career but also for the keen expository insights he brings to the interpretation of Ephesians in the context of university course work. As the introductory essays suggest and the lectures themselves exhibit, Barth was ambivalent, perhaps even uneasy, about the utility and appropriateness of historical-critical methods for uncovering the substance of the New Testament texts. In regard to Ephesians, Barth was, to be sure, thoroughly familiar with the contemporaneous discussions of the critical questions concerning issues such as the authorship, situation, and date of the letter, and of the relationship of Ephesians to the other texts in the Pauline corpus. However, in Barth's comments on the epistle, such historical and philological work is subordinated to the concern of hearing the apostolic testimony afresh. For Barth, the yield of good critical research into the biblical texts is the elucidation of the message of Scripture so that the significance of that message is received by hearers in the present. But exegesis can only *support* the communication of the message; it can never be said to *establish* it. God alone is the one who addresses us through the voice of Scripture. The extent to which Barth successfully negotiated the distinction between the speaking God and Scripture's voice, between the two horizons of the text, and between the often competing methodological strategies of critical exegesis and theological interpretation is a matter of ongoing discussion among Barth scholars, researchers in modern theology, and those interested in the theological interpretation of Scripture. The publication of this English edition of the Ephesians lectures sheds new light upon Barth's contribution to theology's perennial labor of sorting out these issues.

Theological commitments evident throughout Barth's writings from the Göttingen period animate his interpretation of the letter. In particular, we find Barth devoting considerable attention to how, for the Pauline author of Ephesians, the "eschatological character of divine presence and Christian existence"[8] manifests itself in the revelation of the "mystery of [God's] will" (Eph. 1:9)—a concern that is also at the heart of the second edition of *Der Römerbrief*, which Barth was preparing at the same time he delivered these lectures on Ephesians. In addition to providing an incisive analysis of the critical quality of Barth's exegetical moves, Francis Watson's introductory essay offers a comparison of the eschatology that emerges in these lectures to statements found elsewhere in texts from the period, specifically in the Romans commentary and in Barth's lectures on 1 Corinthians 15. Watson's remarks on the cross-currency between Barth and Rudolf Bultmann during the early 1920s are bound to inspire further investigation, as the relationship between Barth and Bultmann is critical for understanding the ascendancy of eschatological and apocalyptic themes in German theology between the wars.

John Webster takes up these themes as well, framing the eschatology of the Göttingen period beneath the broader heading of the relation between God and creatures. Webster shows, among other insights, that Barth's posture vis-à-vis the text of Ephesians as a historical document reflects his thesis that the God who speaks and the creatures who hear remain distinct even while meeting in the event of revelation. The apostolic texts are caught up in the communicative act of God's self-disclosure, and thus the exegete's critical exchanges with the literary features of the New Testament documents are subordinate to the task—which is always beyond the exegete's control—of hearing God speak through the texts. This account shores up the notion that Barth's relative lack of interest in historical and philological questions is a thoroughgoingly *theological* decision about the ontology of Scripture and its location and function in the divine economy.

The first critical German edition of the Ephesians lectures appeared only recently in the *Gesamtausgabe* alongside a series of sermons and notes on the epistle from 1919–20 and a parallel presentation of two lecture cycles on James from 1922–23 and 1928–29, respectively.[9] While a translation of the James lectures is long overdue (as are translations of the lecture cycles on 1 John, Colossians, and the Sermon on the Mount, all of which also have yet to appear in German in the *Gesamtausgabe*), the decision was made to proceed with publication of Ephesians independently of other lecture series from the period. We have not included in the present volume a translation of the material on Ephesians from Barth's time in Safenwil, since many of the insights from his sermons and study notes reappear in the Göttingen lectures. In any case, the lectures exhibit a more fulsome engagement with Ephesians than what we find in the documents from the antecedent Safenwil period.

All of this being said, the reader is advised to consider the genre of the literary work at hand prior to advancing into the text. For these are, indeed, *lectures* on Ephesians, intended originally for aural consumption, designed for an audience of degree-seeking students who for the most part were training for public ministry, and prepared in the throes of a transitional period during which the young Barth struggled to orient himself to the demands of "university" theology. Moreover, Barth labored so intensely through the first chapter of the epistle that he was forced to rush through chapters two through six in the single lecture of February 23, 1922. However, although this volume hardly qualifies as a commentary on Ephesians, it is yet a significant contribution to the commentary tradition associated with the letter, as we encounter in these pages one of the great theological minds of the Christian church fully entranced by the ancient text and eager to broadcast its message to his hearers.

The unique circumstances surrounding this publication have required some editorial decisions in need of explanation in this introduction. This is not, as it were, a critical study edition of the Barth text. Rather, the abiding concern met in this publication is to introduce readers to the first English translation of a significant Barth manuscript. As such, the focus of this volume is on the English rendering of the Ephesians lectures. In an effort to keep the text of the translation as close in appearance to Barth's original transcripts as possible, we have used endnotes for citations, cross-references, and annotations and have used footnotes sparingly to mark Barth's own marginal notes and for critical comments on the handwritten manuscripts. The endnotes incorporate translations of materials from the critical notes of volume editor Jörg-Michael Bohnet in *Erklärung des Epheserbriefes W.S. 1921/22* in the *Gesamtausgabe* as well as textual notes from the translator. As per the style suggestions of the

Barth Translators' Seminar, we have retained the German formatting for endnote citations. Barth introduced each unit of Ephesians with the Greek text followed by his own German translation and then referred back to the Greek in his expositions, often without retranslating words and phrases. The English translation mirrors the original text; that is, only the German is rendered in English here, while the Greek remains untranslated. Whenever possible, we have offered translations of other foreign languages, as when Barth quotes from Calvin in the original French. Biblical cross-references in parentheses are from Barth's handwritten manuscript; those in brackets were inserted into the critical edition by the editor. While we have made efforts to provide a gender-neutral translation, there are instances where it was deemed necessary to translate *Mensch* as "man," even when referring to a human individual generically. Likewise, the translation follows the German original in the gender of pronouns and in language for deity.

We have broken up the text of the lectures into four main portions corresponding to Barth's own division of his pedagogical labors. He followed a standard commentary convention of conceiving chapter one of the letter as consisting of three units of material: the epistolary introduction (1:1–2), a single complex Greek sentence extending through twelve verse divisions that Barth refers to as the great "doxology" (1:3–14), and the elaboration of the author's prayers for the letter's original recipients (1:15–23). Within each of these units, we have demarcated the individual lectures by including the dates of delivery.

We are pleased to include remarks on the translation by Ross M. Wright, who frames the production of the English text within the context of his own work on Barth's early theology, provides further commentary on the origins of the lectures, and offers clarification of technical details concerning his English rendition.

Kaitlyn Dugan, curator of the Barth Collection at Princeton Theological Seminary, offered her expertise at several key junctures during the life of this project and helped the Baker Academic team secure permissions for the striking cover image of Barth from 1925. Hans-Anton Drewes, formerly of the Karl Barth-Archiv in Basel, offered enthusiastic support of the project during the earliest phases. His successor Peter Zocher mediated some early correspondence with the publisher of the German edition, Theologischer Verlag Zürich (TVZ), granted permission for Wright to reuse for the translator's preface material that had previously appeared in an edition of the Archiv's newsletter, and supplied the photographs of Barth's handwritten manuscripts. Niklaus Peter, a member of the Karl-Barth Stiftung, read the translation at the request of TVZ and offered a handful of suggestions for improvment. It was a pleasure to work with Lisa Briner and her team at TVZ to sort out the contract and other legal arrangements. Wright and Francis Watson read through this introductory piece and offered helpful comments. David Chao of the Barth Translators' Seminar provided a summary of the Seminar's style protocols. The contents of the volume were greatly enhanced by David Cramer and Melisa Blok, who joined the editorial team at Baker Academic just before this project entered the production queue.

Barth's *Epistle to the Ephesians* turned out to be my final opportunity to work with my erstwhile *Doktorvater*, John Webster, who passed away unexpectedly on Wednesday, May 25, 2016. His introductory essay, which he delivered to me on the last day of March 2016, is one of his final original pieces. From what I have been able to gather, it also is his last word on Barth, with whose thought he had wrestled his entire career. I had seen John in St Andrews just weeks prior to his death, and on that occasion he shared some constructive comments on the translation of the lectures and on these prefatory remarks. John was actively involved in this project from the very beginning, lending his imprimatur to the publication during the acquisitions phase, eagerly agreeing to pen the essay in spite of his hectic writing schedule, and liberally offering encouragement, advice, and feedback as the manuscript materialized. This project would not have been possible without John's constant support, generosity, and good humor.

# Translating Barth's Ephesians Lectures

Ross M. Wright

Barth delivered his exegetical lectures on Ephesians as he made the transition from the pulpit in Safenwil to the podium in Göttingen. They reveal his theological concerns at the time as well as his determination to read and interpret Scripture as a church theologian. The exposition consists of a detailed exegesis of the Greek text of Ephesians 1:1–23, originally delivered as thirteen lectures, including a summary of Ephesians 2–6 in the final lecture. Because Barth delivered the lectures shortly after completing his *Epistle to the Romans*, it is not surprising to find significant continuity between the two works. For example, readers acquainted with the Romans commentary will recognize signature dialectical expressions, such as "God is God" and "the impossible becomes possible."[1] Likewise, distinctive philosophical concepts from the earlier work appear here: Søren Kierkegaard's notion of "indirect speech" and Franz Overbeck's concept of "the original" (*Ursprung*) to describe the creature's relationship to God. However, the Ephesians lectures also reveal Barth breaking new ground. The theme of the knowledge of God is far more prominent here than in *Romans*, partly because of Barth's engagement with Calvin (he was preparing the 1922 Calvin lectures while delivering the Ephesians exposition) but also because of the prominence of γνῶσις in the text that was before him. Calvin's influence is evident as well in Barth's careful attention to the grammatical, philological, and structural details of the biblical text. Describing Calvin's "objective study" of the Bible, Barth notes in the Calvin lectures: "We can learn from Calvin what it means to stay close to the text, to focus with tense attention on what is actually there . . . , to track down every detail . . . , to stick with the text and to follow wherever it leads."[2] Accordingly, in these lectures on Ephesians, Barth manages to maintain traction with the biblical text as he explores its contemporary meaning.

What kind of exegesis is Barth attempting in the Ephesians lectures? Barth used the term *Erklärung* to describe this particular genre of biblical interpretation and to distinguish it from *Kommentar* or formal commentary.[3] His explication of the text follows the *lectio continua* format. Two reading strategies are evident throughout the lectures. One move consists of grammatical, philological, and structural analysis. In this posture, Barth stands at the podium with the Nestle edition of the Greek New Testament before him and at his disposal an array of modern critical commentaries and New Testament introductions by Dibelius, Jülicher, Weiß, von Soden, Kühl, Harnack, Holzmann, Meyer, and Beck in addition to Luther's commentaries on Ephesians and Calvin's *Opera Selecta*. At this point the exposition resembles a lively conversation as Barth takes his place in the interpretive tradition. Scholarly debate *about* the text, however, is kept to a minimum in order to maintain focus on the text itself. In a second interpretive move, Barth deploys various forms of "ingenious" paraphrase (Bultmann's locution) to reexpress the meaning of the text.[4] At this point he relies on dogmatic categories, dialectical language, and philosophical concepts to explore the text's entailments for present Christian existence. Chiefly, however, he uses intratextual allusions to create a web of biblical associations, which reexpress the meaning of the passage within the larger context of God's saving purposes.[5] Along the way, the lectures crackle with direct address, admonitions about the ministry ("Think about the meaning of the pastoral vocation to which you aspire"),[6] and polemics with faculty members ("Is [the resurrection of Christ] 'only a picture'?"[7]—referring to a lecture delivered the previous day by Walter Bauer). In short, Barth adopts in the Ephesians lectures a form of theological discourse that allows him to engage with issues of New Testament scholarship while honoring the *kerygmatic* nature of the biblical text.

Barth's primary concern in the work of exegesis was to listen to the *Sache* or subject matter of the text. He likened this activity to listening for the sound of someone scratching on the wall, as if from within a prison cell.[8] He was always trying to find a way to allow that voice to be heard, returning to the same text repeatedly, listening afresh and in new ways. In his 1921–22 reading of Ephesians, verse 1:3 emerges as the interpretive key to everything that follows: "Blessed be God, the Father of our Lord Jesus Christ, who has blessed us with every spiritual blessing, in heaven, in Christ." This verse, he notes, "sets the tone for the entire epistle."[9] It witnesses to the divine action, which proceeds from God, sets the creature in motion, and directs the creature to the glory of God. In the following paraphrase of the verse, he summarizes this movement and states the exposition's main theme: "We are created *by* God, from whom we come [*von Gott her*] and *for* God, toward whom we are moving [*auf Gott hin*]. We *are standing* on the ground of the *beneplacitum Dei*; we *are moving* toward the goal of the *gloria Dei*. The knowledge of God is the *presupposition*, and the knowledge of God is the *goal* of all human being, having, and doing, including our present speaking and hearing of divine things!"[10] This theme reflects two of Barth's central theological concerns during the early period: to establish divine prevenience as the basis for the creature's encounter with God and to map out the relationship between divine sovereignty and human freedom.[11] We should understand Barth's approach to Ephesians in light of this concern. He reads Ephesians 1:3 as an indication of the movement from divine action to creaturely existence, and the exposition of the text of the epistle is an attempt to trace this movement.

My translation of Barth's lectures on Ephesians from 1921 to 1922[12] is designed to enable the reader to "hear" the lectures as his students heard them.[13] The Greek text of Ephesians is retained, in accordance with Barth's delivery, demonstrating how his translation conveys crucial interpretive and exegetical moves.[14] Latin and French citations are also included in the body of the text, with standard English translations provided in the endnotes. Where no standard translation exists, I provide my own. The German text is provided at points to inform the translation. In the endnotes, Barth's sources are identified and full bibliographical information is provided, including the standard English edition of translated works. Again, where no standard translation of a German quotation is available, I provide my own.

Vladimir Nabokov warns in "The Art of Translation" that translators can commit three types of transgressions. The first and least egregious consists of "errors due to ignorance or misguided knowledge." The second and more serious is the practice of omitting words or phrases that are obscure: the translator simply "accepts the blank look that his dictionary gives him." The worst degree of turpitude, however, is when a piece is "planished and patted into such a shape" as to conform to the prejudices of the imagined readers.[15] My hope is that the errors of this translation fall into the first category and that readers whose knowledge of German is superior to mine will forgive the "errors due to ignorance or misguided knowledge." To avoid Nabokov's third and worst degree of turpitude, I have made every effort to preserve Barth's juxtaposition of lively, direct address with long, serpentine sentences that negotiate considerable technical exegetical detail. Barth made large demands on his listeners, and I have tried to resist the temptation to simplify the lectures or polish them into shape to conform to my own prejudices. I hope that the translation conveys something of the complexity and rhetorical power of Barth's lectures. In the course of translating them, I have often felt as if I were in the lecture hall, hearing Barth hold forth.

The demands of weekly sermon preparation drew me first to Barth's theology and subsequently to his expository courses on the New Testament. If I had to identify a single way in which this project has changed my approach to exegesis and preaching, it would be the influence of Barth's confidence in Scripture as the *viva vox dei*, the medium through which God makes God's presence known—or, to express the matter differently, his confidence in the *Sache* of the text to establish contact with the listeners, as opposed to relying on personal anecdotes or rhetorical flair. Barth's confidence in the text to refer the reader to the divine voice of God has sent me back to the work of exegesis with renewed confidence in the eloquence or *claritas* of the word of God.

This first published English translation of Barth's Ephesians lectures has been made possible by the enthusiastic support of the editor, Dave Nelson, who recognized their importance early on. Ken Oakes, who read the translation and the German text, saved me from a number of embarrassing errors, tracked down several of Barth's obscure Swiss allusions, and—on the basis of his intimate knowledge of Barth's 1921 *Römerbrief*—pointed out a number of places where the translation needed to reflect the dialectical language and style from this period of Barth's development. Thanks to Good Shepherd Episcopal Church (Richmond), where I serve as rector, I enjoyed a sabbatical in fall 2012 at the University of the South in Sewanee, Tennessee, where I had the opportunity to revise the translation.

An earlier version of this translation was submitted as my PhD dissertation at the University of St Andrews in 2007. The project would not have been possible without the encouragement and support of Hans-Anton Drewes, former head of the Karl Barth-Archiv in Basel. Prior to the appearance of the German edition, he kindly consented to the use of the typescript of Barth's handwritten manuscript, on which the German edition is based, and provided invaluable guidance along the way, including a warm welcome to the Barth-Archiv in July 2004 and an invitation to participate in the Karl Barth *Tagung* in Leuenberg, Switzerland. He also read the version of the translation that appears here and made valuable suggestions, particularly about Barth's use of the phrase "the idea of God." Mark Elliott allowed portions of the text to be discussed in a translation study group at the University of St Andrews and offered suggestions, which have been incorporated in the translation. Gisela Kreglinger, a colleague at St Andrews, read several portions of the translation and made valuable suggestions possible only for a native German speaker. My PhD supervisor, Alan Torrance, believed in the project from the beginning and provided the encouragement and guidance necessary for its completion. The late John Webster, then of the University of Aberdeen, alerted me to the importance of Barth's expository lectures at the Barth-Bonhoeffer Conference in 2000 and provided detailed guidance in the translation and interpretation of Barth's lectures during the completion of the dissertation. A grant from the Russell Trust permitted important archival work in Basel.

The publication of Barth's Ephesians lectures is the culmination of a project that began in 2003. During this time my wife, Lynda, and our sons, Ross, Elliott, and Owen, have sacrificed much to support me in the project. Their love and support have made it possible, and therefore my translation of this theological reflection on the praise of God is dedicated to them.

# Barth, Ephesians, and the Practice of Theological Exegesis

Francis Watson

During the first year of his appointment to a chair of Reformed theology in Göttingen (1921/22), Karl Barth delivered a series of thirteen lectures on Paul's Letter to the Ephesians—six before the break for Christmas and the New Year, seven after it. On the manuscript of his last lecture before Christmas, Barth has written in pencil the words *Klage: zu langsam* ("Complaint: too slow!").[1] A student evidently has objected that, almost halfway through a lecture series supposedly devoted to the whole of the Pauline letter, Barth has gotten no further than Ephesians 1:4. The tempo does increase somewhat in the six lectures that followed the New Year, which take Barth and his audience to the end of the first chapter; a final lecture conducts a rapid survey of Ephesians 2–6. This is, then, essentially an exposition of the first chapter of Ephesians. The pace is slow not because Barth incorporates a mass of exegetical or historical detail but because time and space are needed for him to achieve his fundamental aim, which is to *defamiliarize* the time-honored Pauline vocabulary. In his comments on the letter's opening in verses 1–3, familiar terms such as "apostle" and "will of God," "saints" and "faithful," "grace" and "peace" are dismantled and re-created in a form that emphasizes their orientation away from human religious conviction and experience as conventionally understood toward a God who is always other than our imaginings of him. In using such words, we do not know what we are saying. Paradoxically, it is in the disillusioning awareness of that not-knowing that a true knowledge of God and of ourselves in relation to God may be and must be attained.

At about the time of the student's complaint, Barth's commentary on Romans appeared in its definitive second edition, dated 1922 but actually published shortly before Christmas 1921.[2] Here the first edition is comprehensively rewritten, but Barth retained his original preface so that the work still opens with a resounding contrast between a historical understanding of Paul as a child of his time who addressed his contemporaries and a theological interpretation that unfolds the significance of what he said for the present.[3] The historical-critical method of modern biblical scholarship has its place, no doubt, but the theological interpreter must have quite other priorities. While Barth defends himself against the charge that he is an "enemy of historical criticism" in the preface to the new edition,[4] there is virtually no overlap between his Romans commentary and other contemporary commentaries on the same text. The difference is in part the product of different institutional settings. Barth wrote both editions of his Romans commentary as a minister of the Swiss Reformed Church, not in a university context. While he has a theologically educated readership in view, Barth's prioritizing of the Paul who speaks to us today over the Paul who addressed his own contemporaries reflects an ecclesial setting in which the Bible is the primary basis for preaching and instruction. By the time the book was published, however, Barth had left his Swiss parish and reentered the world of the German university. The question is whether and how far Barth's interpretative practice will adapt to the new setting. Will he interpret Ephesians along the same lines as Romans, or has he moved on? Will he continue to distance himself from the "historical" orientation that he believes determines and limits modern biblical scholarship?

## I

Barth devotes around half of his first lecture (delivered on November 10, 1921) to the question of the authorship of Ephesians, prompted to do so by the epistle's very first word: "Paul" (Eph. 1:1).[5] The text presents itself as the work of Paul. But was he really its author, or did a later disciple compose it in Paul's name after the apostle's death? At the outset Barth makes it clear that this issue is for him a venture into alien territory, that of "historical-critical research of the Bible," which he claims (with some exaggeration) has devoted more time and energy to the authorship question raised by the text's first word than to all its other words put together.[6] While making no claim to originality, Barth summarizes competently the claim that the close relationship of Ephesians to Colossians on the one hand and the absence of characteristic Pauline themes such as the parousia on the other make Pauline authorship improbable.[7] Barth finds this claim unconvincing on empirical grounds: we know from our own experience that a single author may draw extensively from an earlier work in composing a later one and that differences of style and subject matter may be very considerable over the course of an author's career. Overall, there is insufficient reason to conclude that the author of this text was *not* Paul, and Barth is gratified to find that current scholarly opinion has backed away somewhat from Henrich J. Holtzmann's confident denial of Pauline authorship thirty years earlier.[8]

The authorship issue is a staple feature of New Testament introduction (*Einleitung*), the scholarly genre in which one seeks to establish the basic historical facts about a text—who wrote it, when, where, and why—before proceeding to exegesis proper. The second such issue, again discussed by Barth, is that of the addressees of Ephesians.[9] According to the fourth-century codices Sinaiticus and Vaticanus as originally written, Paul's letter was addressed "to the saints who are also faithful in Christ Jesus" (Eph. 1:1). Although these manuscripts entitle this text "To the Ephesians" (*Pros Ephesious*), there was no reference to the Ephesian church within the text itself until the words "at Ephesus" were inserted by later editors: "to the saints who are *at Ephesus*, also faithful in Christ Jesus." A further complication is that Marcion's edition of Paul's Letters entitles this text "To the Laodiceans," a title probably suggested by the reference in Colossians 4:16 to a letter exchange between Colossae and Laodicea. Tertullian accuses Marcion of falsifying only the title of this work and not the text itself, and the words "at Ephesus" were therefore absent from Tertullian's text of Paul as well as Marcion's.[10] The evidence might suggest that a general Pauline or post-Pauline letter was originally addressed "to the saints who are also faithful in Christ Jesus" without any reference to Ephesus; that the title "To the Ephesians" was attached when this text was incorporated into the earliest Pauline letter collection; that Marcion substituted the title "To the Laodiceans" under the influence of Colossians 4:16; and that the words "in Ephesus" were later interpolated into the text itself. That the letter originally lacked any specific connection to Ephesus is confirmed by the fact that the author has *heard about* his addressees' faith in the Lord Jesus but does not know them in person (Eph. 1:15). According to Acts, Paul had spent two whole years in Ephesus (Acts 19:10; cf. 1 Cor. 15:32; 16:8).

Like father, like son. Barth's presentation of these critical issues is indebted to his father Fritz, whose *Einleitung in das Neue Testament* includes a seven-page discussion of the authorship and addressees of Ephesians.[11] Two new posthumous editions of this work were published in 1921, and Karl Barth recommends that his students consult it alongside that of Adolf Jülicher for further discussion of the authorship question.[12] For both Barths, Pauline authorship of Ephesians is put into question neither by the relationship to Colossians nor by distinctive linguistic features or theological emphases. In Ephesians as in Colossians, says Fritz, "it is the aging Paul who speaks, not in the lively polemical manner of the *Hauptbriefen* but as an isolated individual meditating on ideas that span the entire world," and who "knows how to find new language for new ideas."[13] For Karl likewise, "Ephesians is the product of the elderly Paul."[14] Fritz views Ephesians as a circular letter, and for Karl too this seems the "least improbable" solution, even if it is not entirely satisfactory.[15]

Yet this convergence between the two theological generations masks a profound difference. At the close of his foreword, Fritz Barth expresses the hope that his moderately conservative approach to New Testament scholarly issues "may, in these wild and confused times, help to establish the reader on the eternal foundation!"[16] In contrast, his son emphasizes that he has little interest in such matters, that he engages with them only "to fulfill all righteousness" given his new academic context, and that we are to observe the rule (which Barth ascribes to Bengel) *Noli quaerere quis scripserit sed quid scriptum est* ("Do not ask about who wrote but about what is written").[17] Excessive focus on introductory questions about who wrote to whom is said to be characteristic of "the era of historical-critical research of the Bible, which has certainly not yet run its course."[18] Dissatisfied with the debate about the addressees of Ephesians in spite of his partial agreement with his father, Barth winds up his presentation in harshly polemical vein: "Because of the inherent problems, the older theologians at any rate avoided extravagant claims about either their methods or their conclusions."[19]

Why this sharp opposition between *quis scripserit* (the historical question) and *quid scriptum est* (the theological question)? The obvious but superficial answer is that Barth is reacting against the "liberal theology" of which he had once been a devotee and that he opposes "historical criticism" only insofar as it is pressed into the service of a Schleiermacherian theology of "religious experience" or fails to engage with the question of God. Yet Barth's version of the history/theology divide remains puzzling, all the more so as it remained essentially intact throughout his long career and continues to be influential among some advocates of a "theological interpretation of Scripture." In the case of a New Testament letter, the relationship between author and addressees is an explicit feature of the text itself, establishing at the outset the communicative situation presupposed in the letter as a whole. It is not clear why this aspect of the text should be so emphatically downgraded or why those who attempt to engage with it should be caricatured as mere antiquarians using unreliable methods to reach uncertain answers to unimportant questions.

Barth's radical subordination of *quis*-type questions is the negative corollary of his hermeneutical commitment to a "contemporaneity" (*Gleichzeitigkeit*) with Paul that would enable us to hear Jesus Christ bearing witness to himself in and through the words of his apostle. Thus the object (*quid* or *Gegenstand*) of the apostolic testimony becomes its speaking subject.[20] The communicative event that occurs between Paul (or "Paul") and his stated addressees is eclipsed by a communicative event between the risen Christ and ourselves; the Pauline text is transposed into direct address to later readers of the sixteenth or twentieth or twenty-first century. Can we and should we so easily efface the first-century textual artifact and its explicit communicative context? We might imagine a question to that effect posed by the elder Barth to his remarkable son. First-century historical roots may be theologically significant precisely as such. Indeed, the younger Barth's decision to discuss the standard introductory issues at all—in spite of all the rhetorical self-distancing from them—may suggest that he too is aware of their potential significance.

## II

The concern that Paul's text should again be heard as contemporary address is as clear in the Ephesians lectures as in the Romans commentary, published in its second edition as the lectures were under way. As one would expect, there is considerable overlap in Barth's readings of the two Pauline texts. As in every letter in the Pauline corpus, the identification of the sender and the recipients is followed by a theological variation on traditional greeting formulas: "Grace to you and peace from God our Father and the Lord Jesus Christ" (Eph. 1:2). Barth's discussion of the "peace" here referred to echoes the treatment of Romans 5:1 in his commentary: "Therefore, being justified by faith, we have peace with God through our Lord Jesus Christ."[21] In both cases Barth insists that this is a peace that follows a war: not a state of mind but a *Friedensschluss*, a peace agreement in which the divine victory over the rebellious human being is acknowledged.[22] (Barth's original German readers or hearers may have sensed an allusion here to the Peace Treaty or *Friedensvertrag* of Versailles, ratified just two years earlier, in which the dawning of peace was accompanied by the trauma of defeat and loss.) In both cases Barth rejects the claim that the peace in question is a "feeling" (*Gefühl*) or experience in which the heart is strangely warmed; in reality, this peace is the recognition of the gulf that divides, yet paradoxically unites, the holy creator and the sinful creature. The antipietist polemic is on both occasions reinforced, somewhat tendentiously, by the same quotation from Calvin, who states that the peace of God is "the opposite of any capricious, carnal certainty."[23] In a pair of almost identical sentences, Barth twice insists that the person who has peace with God is characterized as one who *waits* in *hope*, as if with empty hands, rather than possessing through faith.[24] In the commentary, this point is motivated by the Pauline ἔχομεν, "we have," which might be taken to imply a state of secure possession until subjected to Barth's deconstructive dialectic. Later in the Ephesians lectures this concern will resurface again in connection with Ephesians 1:7, where the problematic ἔχομεν refers now to "redemption through [Christ's] blood" rather than "peace with God." What we have is what we hope for.[25]

More significant than these similarities between the Romans commentary and the Ephesians lectures is the shift in the relation of the interpreter to the scriptural text. The Barth of the commentary finds in Paul's text the basis for an extended series of polemical meditations on themes evoked by the text. There is little attempt to substantiate these meditations by backward reference to the text or by appeal to other related texts: the phrase cited at the start of a comment (in this case, "we have peace with God") is a point of departure, and the return to the text occurs only as Barth moves on to the following phrase (here "through our Lord Jesus Christ").[26] Although larger blocks of text are cited, the commentary is focused almost exclusively on smaller units—from single sentences down to single words. There is little or no attempt to analyze the structure of a Pauline argument, for the focus is not on the Pauline text as such but on the divine reality to which it bears witness. The aim is, as Barth states in his second preface, that the text itself should become "transparent," a medium that enables us to view the divine reality that lies beyond it only insofar as it becomes invisible.[27] The very purpose of this commentary, then, is to *erase* the text in its relative solidity as an artifact—or rather to show how, in view of its relation to its unique object, it solicits its own erasure. It is in line with this extraordinarily bold hermeneutical claim that Barth can eliminate the distinction between himself as interpreter and Paul as author: the interpreter gripped by the text's subject matter can "almost forget" that he is not its author.[28]

In the Ephesians lectures, this hermeneutic of textual self-effacement has receded. The free theological meditations of the commentary are still present in the lectures, but they are accompanied by a quite different interpretative practice, absent from the commentary: in a word, by *exegesis*. The difference is signaled not only by the use of the Greek text but also by the fact that it is frequently cited *within* Barth's comments on particular words or phrases. The movement is no longer *away from* the text but *around* it. Barth's Ephesians is not transparent; it bears witness, but it does not make itself invisible any more than Matthias Grünewald's *John the Baptist* does as he gestures toward the Lamb of God who takes away the sin of the world—a figure in whom Barth already sees an icon of the biblical witness.[29]

In the practice of exegesis it is assumed that small-scale interpretative decisions are integral to the attempt to articulate the theological substance of a text; and this is an assumption that the Barth of the Ephesians lectures now appears to accept. Thus, according to the Pauline author, God "chose us in [Christ] before the foundation of the world that we should be holy and blameless before him" (Eph. 1:4), and God also "foreordained us for adoption through Jesus Christ" (Eph. 1:5). Between the two parallel statements stands the phrase "in love" (ἐν ἀγάπῃ). Does this phrase point back to what precedes it? In that case God chose us to be holy and blameless before him *in love*. This love presumably would be our own, viewed as the comprehensive context of the holy and blameless life that God intends for us.[30] Or should "in love" be connected to what follows? Was it "in love" that God "foreordained us for adoption through Jesus Christ"? Such a love would then be the divine love that motivates adoption through Jesus Christ. Which is it? The translators are divided on this matter. The King James Version's "that we should be holy and without blame before him in love" is reproduced in the Revised Version with a modest emendation only of "blame" to "blemish." The Revised Standard Version goes the other way: God chose us to be "holy and blameless before him" and "destined us *in love* to be his sons through Jesus Christ." If these revisers had followed the Greek word order, the text would have read, "*in love* destining us," and it was perhaps the slight awkwardness of this wording that led the next generation of revisers to revert to the King James Version for the New Revised Standard Version reading: "just as he chose us in Christ to be holy and blameless before him *in love*." In one sense, this is a decision of minor importance. Both readings make good theological sense, and one might decide that both are equally valid. In another sense, an exegetical decision such as this is anything but trivial. If the text is to have its intended effect as an act of communication, appropriate construal of its words, phrases, and sentences is important—not least, as Augustine pointed out, for the lector preparing to read a scriptural passage in a liturgical setting.[31] In reflecting on what it might mean to be holy and blameless before God, we need to know whether the phrase "in love" does or does not serve as an interpretive key to that holy and blameless way of life.

Modern editors of the Greek New Testament face the same problem as translators. The ancient manuscripts on which they rely generally lack punctuation and even spaces between words. In the great fourth-century uncial Codex Sinaiticus, to which Barth refers briefly in his second lecture,[32] the relevant passage is formatted as follows:

ΚΑΘΩCΕΞΕΛΕΞΑΤΟ
ΗΜΑCΕΝΑΥΤΩΠΡΟ
ΚΑΤΑΒΟΛΗCΚΟCΜΟΥ
ΕΙΝΑΙΗΜΑCΑΓΙΟΥC
ΚΑΙΑΜΩΜΟΥCΚΑ
ΤΕΝΩΠΙΟΝΑΥΤΟΥ
ΕΝΑΓΑΠΗΠΡΟΟΡΙ
CΑCΗΜΑCΕΙCΥΙΟ
ΘΕCΙΑΝΔΙΑΙΥΧΥΕΙC
ΑΥΤΟΝ . . .[33]

In presenting the Greek New Testament to modern readers, editors make use of supplementary aids to comprehension such as lowercase letters, word division, punctuation, and verse enumeration. The present exegetical issue hangs on where the editor places the comma. In Eberhard Nestle's popular *Novum Testamentum Graece*, used by Barth,[34] the first two editions punctuate the key words as follows:

> . . . εἶναι ἡμᾶς ἁγίους καὶ ἀμώμους κατενώπιον αὐτοῦ ἐν ἀγάπῃ, προορίσας ἡμᾶς εἰς υἱοθεσίαν . . .
>
> . . . that we should be holy and blameless before him in love, foreordaining us for adoption . . .[35]

In the third edition, however, dating from 1901, Nestle has changed his mind about how the passage is to be punctuated:

> . . . εἶναι ἡμᾶς ἁγίους καὶ ἀμώμους κατενώπιον αὐτοῦ, ἐν ἀγάπῃ προορίσας ἡμᾶς εἰς υἱοθεσίαν . . .
>
> . . . that we should be holy and blameless before him, in love foreordaining us for adoption . . .

Barth agrees with the more recent editions of the Nestle text that "in love" refers to the God who foreordains and opens a new sense-unit: ἐν ἀγάπῃ προορίσας ἡμᾶς . . .[36] He considers that the link between "holy and blameless" and "in love" would be highly unusual and that a reference to divine rather than human love is more in keeping with the emphasis of the passage as a whole. This enables him to make the theological point that will prove so significant for the *Church Dogmatics*, namely, that the God who predestines is as such also the God who loves. What is hermeneutically significant, however, is the simple fact that Barth discusses the alternative exegetical option. If the Pauline statement is taken to read, "that we should be holy and blameless before him *in love*," supporting evidence might be found in Romans 8:28, where "those who love God" are also "those who are called according to his purpose," so that, as Barth puts it, "human creature's love for God" is viewed as "the correlate of divine election."[37] A parallel from the immediate context in Ephesians 1 may also be found in the retrospective ἐν-clause in verse 8, where it is said that God made his grace to abound for us "in all wisdom and understanding." According to Barth, that phrase cannot point ahead to verse 9, "making known to us the mystery of his will."[38] Arguing an exegetical point on the basis of analogies in the immediate context or in related texts is, of course, standard exegetical practice, which can also be adapted—as here—to serious exegetical options with which one disagrees. Barth's discussion of this point displays exegetical competence rather than any special insight. What is noteworthy is that he here accepts the traditional assumption that interpretation must begin by establishing what the text does and does not say. At points such as this, Barth does *not* proclaim that the theological interpreter of Scripture must rise above the pedantries and minutiae of normal exegetical practice in order to engage a theme that lies beyond the words of the text. We cannot have the theme apart from the words, and we cannot have the words without grammar and syntax.

## III

After the initial greeting, Ephesians opens with a doxology: "Blessed be the God and Father of our Lord Jesus Christ, who has blessed us with every spiritual blessing in the heavenly realms in Christ, as he chose us in him . . ." (Eph. 1:3–4). The spiritual blessings are further elaborated in a single long sentence extending to verse 14; they include foreordination, adoption, grace, redemption, forgiveness, revelation, sealing, promise, and the Holy Spirit. Such listing of benefits for which God is to be blessed or praised is characteristic of the New Testament's doxologies: "Blessed be the Lord God of Israel, for he has visited and redeemed his people . . ." (Luke 1:68; cf. 2 Cor. 1:3–4; 1 Pet. 1:3–5). The syntax of the Ephesian doxology is uniquely tortuous, however, as illustrated by the opening words of each verse in the KJV rendering:

> [4]according as he hath chosen . . . , [5]having predestinated us . . . , [6]to the praise . . . , [7]in whom we have redemption . . . , [8]wherein he hath abounded . . . , [9]having made known . . . [10]that in the dispensation . . . , [11]in whom also . . . , [12]that we should . . . , [13]in whom ye also . . . [14]which is the earnest . . .

A similar effect is created by Luther's German translation, to which Barth here refers.[39]

According to Barth, a translation that preserves the structure of this labyrinthine sentence serves only to make it incomprehensible. A key is needed, and Barth takes up the suggestion of Martin Dibelius's commentary on the shorter Pauline Epistles (1913) that such a key is to be found in the recurrent use of the formula “in Christ” or “in whom” (= “in him”).[40] God has blessed us *in Christ*. That is to say:

> [4]*In him* he chose us, before the foundation of the world was laid . . .
> [7]*In him* we have redemption through his blood . . .
> [11]*In him* we have also become heirs . . .
> [13]*In him* you also, who have heard the word of truth . . .

Thus the movement of thought is from Jesus Christ as our election (vv. 4–6) to Jesus Christ as our liberation (vv. 7–10) to Jesus Christ as our hope (vv. 11–12) to Jesus Christ as our sealing (vv. 13–14).[41]

This concern to analyze the structure of a section of text is again a standard feature of normal exegetical practice, one that is almost entirely absent from the Romans commentary. Also noteworthy here is Barth’s explicit dependence on a contemporary exegete. Dibelius was twice cited earlier as a representative of the “historical-critical research of the Bible,” the “older theologians” who pride themselves on their “methods” and “conclusions” while generating only uncertainties and hypotheses.[42] Some scholars are sure that Paul did not write Ephesians; others believe that he did; others still remain undecided. Various unsatisfactory theories have been proposed to explain the probable absence of the words “to Ephesus” in Ephesians 1:2. Dibelius, who denies Pauline authorship, argues that the usage of key terms such as σῶμα and μυστήριον differs between Ephesians and Colossians.[43] On the issue of the addressees, Dibelius suggests that ἐν Ἐφέσῳ is a later addition suggested by 2 Timothy 4:12: “Tychicus I sent to Ephesus” (cf. Eph. 6:21).[44] As we have seen, Barth reports these views while distancing himself from them and from the scholarly tradition that (he thinks) grossly exaggerates their significance. So Barth is dismissive of Dibelius and his kind when the letter’s author and addressees are under discussion yet is appreciative of—indeed, grateful for—the exegete’s insights into the text’s structure. Whether Barth is justified in drawing this distinction between historical and exegetical issues is another matter. What is more significant is the tacit acknowledgment that contemporary biblical scholarship is not *exclusively* antiquarian or historical or critical in orientation. It is *also and above all* concerned to make a difficult text readable by analyzing structure, syntax, semantics, and everything else pertaining to what was once called "grammatical" interpretation.[45] The term "historical criticism" does not adequately represent the modern interpretative tradition and its exegetical practice.[46]

In this case, as in others, Barth's theological interpretation arises from his grammatical exegesis. Having clarified the structure of the complex Ephesian doxology, he returns to the fact that in its ancient Greek rather than modern German form it remains a single sentence. Corresponding to its singularity is the single divine act of which it speaks. According to Barth, the many diverse components that make up the sentence are all concerned to articulate a single comprehensive truth, a *kerygma* rather than a set of dogmatic *loci*.[47] That recurrent "in him" calls us to listen for the one Word in the many words, the divine address that reminds us that we stand before God and are claimed by God—the God revealed in Christ as Immanuel, God with us, but as such the *Deus absconditus* who cannot be reduced to our conceptualizations or experiences, even if these seem to be supported by the language of Scripture. Election and predestination, adoption and redemption refer us not to a set of carefully coordinated doctrines, each with its own place within a grand narrative of salvation, but to the existential reality that our life in its totality is subject to the divine address in its origin, its unfolding, and its destiny. In hermeneutical terms, the Pauline text speaks truly of God by speaking indirectly. We cannot dispense with the many words that point to the one Word, but neither can we simply identify the transcendent divine address with its apostolic testimony.

## IV

It is not clear from the Romans commentary that Barth is able to practice exegesis and theology simultaneously. Given that he uses the commentary to construct a theology, it is difficult to see the text-based theological meditations of that work as in any sense exegesis. In contrast, the Ephesians lectures show some signs of rapprochement with conventional exegetical practice, and it is worth reflecting further on the relation between the exegesis and the lectures' radically theological orientation. More successfully perhaps than in the Romans commentary, Barth is able to show that key theological commitments have been read *out of* the Pauline text and not simply imposed on it.

As already noted, Barth is hypersensitive to the possible implications of the Pauline ἔχομεν. We "have" peace with God; we "have" redemption only as those who *hope for* peace and redemption (cf. Rom. 5:1; Eph. 1:7). Contrary to all pietisms, we have only insofar as we acknowledge that we *do not* have. Yet the whole first chapter of Ephesians might seem to refute this willfully paradoxical claim. The introductory doxology seeks to evoke in its hearers or readers a sense of the immeasurable abundance of the spiritual riches bestowed on them. The response that it intends is not sober recognition of disillusioning truth but enthusiastic participation in its own song of praise. For its intended hearers or readers, this overly long and loosely constructed sentence is precisely the vehicle that transports them into the heavenly realms of which the text speaks. From where they stand, there is no dialectical countering of the divine giving by a divine withholding.

Or so it might seem. Barth, however, reads the text as something other than an expression of pietistic fervor. He notes how, after introducing himself and identifying his addressees, Paul converts into a prayer the greetings formulas that conventionally open Greek or Jewish letters: "Grace to you and peace from God our Father and the Lord Jesus Christ" (Eph. 1:2).[48] The prayer is followed by the doxological celebration of spiritual riches freely bestowed, yet the fact that the doxology is preceded by prayer remains significant. Grace has indeed been freely bestowed, yet Paul prays that grace may still be bestowed. One does not pray for what one already securely possesses. Grace and peace must *come* to us; they are not simply *there*. The doxology itself does not merely articulate something that its readers already experience; rather, it is a reminder of what they know but are always liable to forget.

If it seems exegetically implausible to read the imposing doxology in the light of the conventional Pauline greeting, Barth can point to the more extensive prayer with which the first chapter of Ephesians closes (1:15–23).[49] Here God is asked to bestow what he has already bestowed according to the doxology. God has poured out upon us "the riches of his grace . . . in all wisdom and understanding" (1:7–8); he has "made known to us the mystery of his will" (1:9). Yet Paul can also pray for his addressees as though they still lacked that revelatory wisdom, understanding, and knowledge, asking that God "may give you a spirit of wisdom and revelation in the knowledge of him" (1:17) and that "the eyes of your heart may be enlightened so that you may know what is the hope of his calling and what are the riches of the glory of his inheritance in the saints" (1:18). Paul does not pray that readers who already know may progress to a still higher grade of knowledge. He asks not that open eyes be opened still wider but that sight be given to the blind. The addressees know but do not yet know. They have been filled yet stand before God with empty hands. In Barth's words, "Any truth that is *not new* does not qualify as God's truth. Likewise, when redemption ceases to be an object of hope and becomes something we possess or consume, it is no longer redemption. . . . Yesterday's discovery must be sought anew today."[50]

This dialectic of having and not-having is characteristic of Barth's early theology. It remains prominent in the first volume of the *Church Dogmatics*, and its echoes are also perceptible throughout the theology of Rudolf Bultmann, whom Barth so strongly influenced in spite of the later distance between them.[51] Yet the dialectic is not simply Barth's own invention. It has a genuinely Pauline basis, not least in the creative tension between the doxology and the prayer that constitutes Ephesians 1—the chapter to which Barth devotes twelve of his thirteen lectures on this letter. It is his overarching theological concerns that enable him to see and to exploit this fundamental feature of the Pauline text. There is nothing that corresponds to this in Dibelius's commentary, which provides a more sustained exegetical discussion than Barth's lectures but lacks his drive toward the one Word beyond the many words of the text. Students attending the lectures would have needed to supplement what they learned from Barth with the exegetical wisdom to be found in a commentary such as Dibelius's if they were to become competent interpreters of the scriptural text and not just ardent disciples of their soon-to-be-famous teacher. Barth cannot justly claim that his theocentric reading is an adequate substitute for the conventional commentary, in which attention to nuance and context is itself a tribute to the text's enduring theological value. Yet his theocentrism can issue in startling exegetical insights that both illuminate the text and disclose its potential to reshape its readers' world.

## V

In the prayer of Ephesians 1:15–19, Paul asks for his readers the capacity to comprehend the divine gift that is theirs and the divine power that has made it possible. In the following verses, the basis for the divine power exercised on their behalf is disclosed: the resurrection of Jesus. Thus, Barth suggests, verses 20–21 answer the implied question of verses 18–19.[52] Indeed, all the diverse soteriological terms employed in this chapter find their origin and rationale in the event in which God raised Jesus from the dead and made him sit at his right hand. As 1 Corinthians 15 confirms, it is this singular divine action that constitutes *das Wesen des Christentums*, the essence of Christianity[53]—and not, for example, the noneschatological core of Jesus's teaching as argued by Harnack in his celebrated book of two decades earlier.[54] In Harnack's account of Christian faith, Pauline christological and eschatological convictions play only a subordinate role. For Barth, what mattered most to the apostle should matter most to us.

Jesus's resurrection, says Barth, is an "unhistorical" event that lies on the boundary between time and eternity: unhistorical but nevertheless an *event* that may be described as an *eternal* event so long as we understand eternity as God's presence within time.[55] Indeed, this is a *bodily* event, for life in time is embodied life, and the resurrection of Jesus is the disclosure of the truth of that embodied life: that it is subject to the divine word of judgment and grace, that in Jesus God draws near to us as the holy one, the creator whose relation to his creatures entails his transcendence.[56] If an interpretation along these lines is utterly inadequate (as it is), it is because the resurrection as the definitive act of God cannot be grasped by any of our normal criteria of intelligibility. Paul *prays* that his readers will have their eyes opened to the transcendent divine power that raised Jesus from the dead because they have no existing capacity to grasp such an event. If the prayer is answered and eyes are indeed opened, the new knowledge will be articulated in negations as much as in affirmations. Here too knowing for Barth is a not-knowing aware of itself as such. A "historical" resurrection would be an event understood within some prior category rather than an event *sui generis*. Whether appeal is made to supernatural causation or to visionary experiences, the divine act is deprived of its mystery. One side of the well-known debate may insist, on the basis primarily of the Gospels' story of the empty tomb, that the resurrection involves the miraculous reanimation of Jesus's corpse. On the other side, the earlier testimony of 1 Corinthians 15 is said to suggest that resurrection faith originated in ecstatic visions of the risen Lord. For Barth, the entire debate is wasted effort that strives in vain to make the invisible visible and to dispel the divine mystery.[57] The less that can be said about the historical basis of resurrection faith, the better. If modern historical research has brought to light the problematic, fragmentary, and contradictory nature of the New Testament's testimony to Jesus's resurrection, that is something for which we must be *grateful*.[58] Human language necessarily fails at this point, and that very failure should be viewed as negative testimony to the transcendence of the divine act.

In this disconcerting reference to modern biblical scholarship in its most iconoclastic vein, Barth may have in mind the work of his slightly older contemporary Rudolf Bultmann, whose appointment to a chair in Marburg in the 1921–22 academic year coincided with Barth's own arrival in Göttingen. Both appointments were occasioned by important and controversial publications: in Barth's case the Romans commentary in its first edition, in Bultmann's *The History of the Synoptic Tradition*. Completed in 1919, Bultmann's first major work was published in April 1921, predating by a few months the second edition of Barth's commentary, published in December of that year as the Ephesians lectures were under way.[59] Barth delivered the lecture devoted to Ephesians 1:20–23 and the resurrection on February 16, 1922. Just two days later, on February 18, he traveled to Marburg to discuss the newly published commentary with Bultmann and his students.[60] Bultmann's lengthy and favorable review of Barth's commentary is well known.[61] Less well known is Barth's appreciation of Bultmann's work on the Synoptic tradition, at least in its general orientation.[62] This work may have been uppermost in his mind when he commended radical historical study of the Gospel resurrection narratives shortly before his Marburg visit. According to Bultmann, all the Gospels' Easter stories are belated attempts to make the incomprehensible comprehensible and the incredible credible.[63] Even the earliest of them, the Markan story of the empty tomb, is a secondary supplement to the Passion Narrative, which is out of step with its literary context and rendered internally inconsistent through the insertion of the reunion-in-Galilee motif (Mark 16:7; cf. 14:28). Easter stories in later Gospels are said to be apologetic legends that seek to validate the resurrection *kerygma* by narrating appearances of the risen Lord. It is analysis of this kind, supported by acute exegetical observation, for which Barth thinks we should be "grateful"—laying special emphasis on the word *dankbar* in his lecture manuscript. Precisely in the failure of their apologetic strategies, these narratives bear witness to an event beyond the reach of narrative or any other means of bringing the unknown into the sphere of the known.

As evidenced in the Ephesians lectures of 1921–22, Barth's relation to the traditions and conventions of biblical scholarship is complex. As we have seen, Barth distances himself from what he (wrongly) regards as extraneous historical questions about author and addressees, yet he devotes significant parts of the earlier lectures to discussing them (I). He works with the Greek text and has internalized the exegete's awareness that small-scale issues of syntax and sense can have major interpretative consequences (II). Equally characteristic of the exegete are Barth's concern to analyze the structure of larger units of text and the willingness to engage with and learn from other exegetes in doing so (III). While theological preoccupations are everywhere to the fore, Barth makes serious and successful attempts to show their grounding within the scriptural text (IV). Barth's radical Paulinism leads him to make unexpected common cause with a scholar already regarded by many as an archenemy of historic Christianity (V). Nearly a century after they were delivered, and from whatever perspective one comes to them, these lectures on Ephesians retain their power to disconcert.

# "A Relation beyond All Relations"

## *God and Creatures in Barth's Lectures on Ephesians, 1921–22*

John Webster

### I

Over the course of his relatively brief but extraordinarily active tenure of the newly founded chair of Reformed theology in Göttingen from 1921 to 1925, Barth lectured in three areas of the theological curriculum: historical theology, dogmatics, and New Testament exegesis. The publication of a good number of the historical and dogmatic lectures in the Barth *Gesamtausgabe* over the last quarter century has made abundantly clear how formative the time in Göttingen proved to be, not only for the decade or so before the appearance of the first volume of the *Church Dogmatics*—during which Barth deepened, clarified, and refined the theological positions that he had begun to adopt in the middle of the Great War as he distanced himself from Herrmann and later liberal Protestantism—but also for his mature work in the three decades in Basel. His teaching in Reformed historical theology led him to acquaint himself more thoroughly with the confessional and theological writings of that tradition—the Heidelberg Catechism, the Reformed confessions, and the works of Calvin, Zwingli, and Schleiermacher[1]—and on that basis to take up a stance toward and formulate his own interpretation of the material in which he was obligated to provide instruction. He quickly identified what he took to be the marks of Reformed theology and Christian practice: astonishment before and responsibility to divine revelation as a present, entirely uncontainable occurrence; commitment to the Scripture principle and corresponding dedication to the task of biblical exegesis and exposition; an eschatological moralism in which divine majesty at one and the same time evokes and relativizes action in the world. In dogmatics, Barth's Göttingen lectures were the beginning of what was to be a lifelong task of setting out a comprehensive account of Christian teaching in a quite different register from that of his teachers, one that required him to reconceive the objects, cognitive principles, and ends of dogmatics and to recast and reorder its various *loci*.[2]

Recognition of the importance of the Göttingen lectures in biblical exegesis has been quite slow, largely because of the unavailability of much of the material: although the lectures on 1 Corinthians 15 were published in 1924,[3] and a revised version of those on Philippians, originally given in 1924 and then delivered in Münster, appeared in 1927,[4] those on James and Ephesians have been published only recently,[5] and those on 1 John, Colossians, and the Sermon on the Mount remain unpublished. Many of the standard accounts of Barth's early work say little of his exegetical labors beyond *The Epistle to the Romans*, and a good deal of the literature on his hermeneutics and exegetical practice confines itself to *Romans* or to the *Church Dogmatics*, though there is increasing recognition of the importance of Barth's study of and teaching about Paul in the decisive phase of his theological development.[6] If the lectures on historical theology were, inter alia, exercises in *ressourcement* and critical retrieval of elements of the Reformed tradition, those on New Testament texts were exercises in commentarial exposition of Christian teaching, setting forth the content of Christian belief neither by free theologizing nor by topical, systematic anatomy but by the attempt to articulate what Barth took to be the matter indicated by the biblical text. This was undertaken on the basis of a conviction that theology is derivative from and governed by exegesis and directed toward exposition. Exegesis and exposition are necessary because they are the activities through which access to biblical instruction is constantly to be sought. As Barth states in a lecture on Calvin,

> The relation to the Bible is a living one. The spring does not flow of itself. It has to be tapped. Its waters have to be drawn. The answer is not already there; we have to ask what it is. The Bible calls for objective study. What is in it is, of course, known already insofar as it is a matter of the relation about which we cannot ask without first knowing it, but because it is a matter of the form and order of this relation in time, we do not yet know what is in the Bible, and, as is unavoidable in time, we have to seek and find this by work. The Bible is thus opened and listened to with a readiness to receive what is not yet known, not for the purpose of finding again what is known already.[7]

Moreover, objectivity in theology—attentiveness to theology's *Sache* in its otherness from the expectations of religious and theological subjectivity—requires constant and concentrated exercise of expectant, untrammeled exegetical intelligence. Barth continues: "This is what gives Calvin's expository skill its first distinctive feature: its extraordinary objectivity. We can learn from Calvin what it means to stay close to the text, to focus with tense attention on what is actually there. Everything else *derives* from this. But it has to derive from *this*. If it does not, then the expounding is not real questioning and readiness to listen."[8]

The lectures on Ephesians were delivered in Barth's first semester in Göttingen, and he was much occupied with this New Testament text in the final period of his pastorate in Safenwil. In a letter to Eduard Thurneysen in March 1918, he reported that he had been studying the text with his confirmation candidates,[9] and from May to September of the following year he delivered a series of sermons on the epistle.[10] Later that same year he produced a translation and brief interpretation of Ephesians, which became the basis for an adult

Bible study in the parish in the following spring. From this emerged a written text, consisting of a translation and notes on the letter, into which are interpolated summaries of the sermons that Barth had earlier delivered.[11] The Göttingen lectures on Ephesians are the culmination of this extended engagement.

The lectures are especially valuable for the light they shed on one of Barth's principal preoccupations in Göttingen (and, arguably, well beyond Göttingen in his mature theology of covenant), namely, the relation between God and creatures. Many of Barth's concerns in that concentrated, vivid period of development turn on that relation: his understanding of history, his eschatology, his theology of the resurrection, his theology of revelation and its associated hermeneutics, his ethics, and his interpretation of the differing emphases of the Lutheran and Reformed wings of the Reformation. In accounts of Barth's early theology, his way of articulating the relation of God and creatures is commonly designated "dialectical." Though Barth himself makes quite frequent appeal to the term, it is probably best to use it sparingly in characterizing his work. Partly this is because the term has been used in rather different ways in some of the controversies in the reception of Barth's writings; partly, again, because its deployment as an overarching interpretive category may inhibit close observation of the variety and scope of what Barth has to say about the relation of God and creatures in the various genres in which he was working.

In the lectures on Ephesians, we can observe Barth's thinking about the matter firsthand. More particularly, we can see him trying to learn from this New Testament text how to think about God's presence to and relation with creatures in rather less starkly oppositional terms than those to which he makes much appeal in the second edition of *The Epistle to the Romans*, completed just as he left Safenwil for Göttingen.

## II

Barth's exegesis of Ephesians presupposes, and occasionally makes explicit, an understanding of the relation between divine communication and the causality of its creaturely media. Though he does not bring to the exercise anything like a comprehensive theology of revelation and Scripture, he does have some working principles to which he turns on those occasions when, in the course of interpreting the text, he thinks himself required to give attention to its origin and its primary speaker.

In his final lecture on the prologue to Ephesians, Barth remarks on this "compendium of the fundamental Pauline framework":

> It offers a glimpse into the unprecedented revolution that must have occurred in the hearts and minds of this group of people in the first century and the impression it must have made upon them—upon both Paul and his readers, whom he considered capable of understanding such ideas! It is impossible on the basis of historical analysis to perceive the essentially imperceptible event that occurred here, or anywhere. . . . However, I hope that I have convinced you that it is possible to enter sympathetically with Paul and not only to see along with Paul but to think along with him at that point where *the subject matter* [*Gegenstand*], *the incommensurable*, *Jesus Christ*, speaks and becomes his own interpreter.[12]

Barth reads Ephesians as an apostolic text, whose origin lies in the attempt on the part of its author to indicate the wholly incommensurable reality and presence of God, and which is now the means whereby its readers are drawn before that reality and presence. The lectures on Ephesians antedate his engagement with the Reformed Scripture principle in lectures on the Reformed confessional writings,[13] and he does not characterize the nature and function of the text by appeal to the theological categories deployed by that principle. Rather, he thinks of the text, in both its origin and its effect, as arising from and indicative of realities that may not be drawn within the regularities of history.

This does not mean that Barth is wholly indifferent to the literary properties of the text. As in the other Göttingen exegetical lectures, the text enjoys a good deal more prominence than it does in either of the first two editions of the *Romans* commentary (despite the fact that both editions are indeed intended to be *commentaries*). If in *Romans* the relation between what the text says and what Barth says that the text says is not always transparent, in Ephesians the governance of the text is much more direct and explicit. The text is not simply the occasion for the articulation of Barth's theological convictions (prompted and informed by the text, perhaps, but not always demonstrably bound by and directed toward it). Rather, the text of Ephesians is that to which Barth attempts to direct his hearers' attention and that whose course he seeks to follow. He does not devote a great deal of time to linguistic, grammatical, and stylistic matters or to a review of exegetical options; his attention is much more gripped by the matter of the text. Nevertheless, what he offers his hearers is not a set of theological variations on topics in Ephesians; it is, rather, theology in exegetical and expository mode.

Barth remains ambivalent, however, toward the value of historical investigation of the text and its provenance for coming to understand its matter. It is important not to attribute to Barth some principled indifference to history or an "antihistorical" attitude, either in reading biblical texts or more generally in historical theology.[14] Barth does consider it necessary to devote some time at the beginning of the lecture series to questions of authorship and recipients, though he does not find such matters engaging, and he concludes his review of the phrase ἐν Ἐφέσῳ early on in the third lecture on a weary note: "I believe that I have discharged my duty by making you aware of all these possibilities, and I leave it to you to decide which of them is the least improbable."[15]

Barth's sense of the restricted applicability and fruitfulness of historical inquiry in biblical interpretation arises from what he takes to be the matter of the text and the communicative act of which the text forms an element. He considers that Ephesians sets before its readers a reality that exceeds historical intelligence, even as it presents itself in a textual form inextricable from (though not wholly exhausted by) historical processes of authorship and reception. Both the matter of the text and the way in which the textual indication of that matter comes into being point to the limits of historical description and explanation.

The matter to which exegetical intelligence is to be directed, on Barth's account, is not simply the historical quantities of the religious lives, situation, or beliefs of its author and original recipients but an "eschatological" reality. If exegesis terminates on some interim reality, it has not run its full course. Lecturing on Ephesians 1:20 ("[God] raised him from the dead") on February 16, 1922, for example, Barth notes that when the author speaks of resurrection, "he means an event . . . that is more nearly impossible and unhistorical than historical. He means the impossible event κατ' ἐξοχήν . . . an event that takes place precisely at the *boundary* between what is possible and what is impossible, what is historical and what is unhistorical, time and eternity."[16] "Boundary" is an important term here: it is not that the matter of Ephesians is transcendent *tout court* but more that—in its difference from the temporal—that matter points beyond itself "in" time, though not as a contingent temporal happening but as the displacement of time, as time's outer edge. What is given in Jesus Christ, Barth says,

> is given in *history*, therefore not as something other than history, removed from history, in addition to history, removed from history—not as a Platonic idea, as popularly conceived. It is given as an idea in the fullest sense, that is, as the idea or conception of *God*, therefore as the origin of all *origins*, the inaccessible in the immediate, the wholly other in the human, the beyond in *this life*. But note: it is given as an *event* in history, as *the other side* of this world, as an event that is in history but not *of* it—not a mere object of history but history's fundamental origin and absolute boundary. This boundary and origin are of a different order than anything that can be explained on *the basis of history* or examined within *the established order of knowledge*, even the most extraordinary and unprecedented event.[17]

Such is the incommensurability of the resurrection that it cannot be grasped through categories such as "miracle" or "vision," which draw the resurrection within the domain of historical experience: "The reality that Paul describes here is not experienced the way we experience anything else. It would be far more faithful to Paul to say that we do not experience it at all."[18] Historical-critical research offers a negative testimony to this: precisely by advertising the contradictions in the biblical accounts of the resurrection, it reveals "just how improbable, implausible, and historically impossible the event is."[19] Similar attempts by Barth to discriminate the matter of the text from anything experientially or historically available and familiar recur throughout the lectures. What he finds himself struggling to articulate to his audience is, quite simply, nonpareil, that to which we cannot stand in any accustomed historical relation.

Something similar is found in the account of the authorship of Ephesians with which Barth opens the lecture series. Starting from the letter's first word, Παῦλος, he gives a brief survey of the *status quaestionis* concerning Pauline authorship, concluding that though he himself "would defend the authenticity" of the letter, he does not "have any great interest in the question," preferring to follow Bengel: *Noli quaerere quis scripserit sed quid scriptum est.*[20] If Bengel is attractive to Barth, it is because to accord priority to *quid scriptum est* is to detach study of the Bible from inquiry into religious personality[21] and instead to devote attention to the revelatory matter of which the Bible is sign and embassy.

There is, doubtless, a certain externality in this account of the relation of the matter of the Bible and its human authorship. The decisiveness with which Barth separates *quis scripserit* from *quid scriptum est* may suggest that the natural properties of the author (e.g., cultural setting; moral, spiritual, and intellectual gifts; virtues and experiences) are not sanctified or caused to serve the presentation of the *res* of the text but are little more than occasion for the acts of another agent, having no instrumental role. On the other hand, it may be that as he tries to dispose himself before the text, Barth is not eliminating or suspending the human author so much as characterizing the kind of human authorial activity that occurs in the sphere of (eschatological) reality in which Ephesians is caught up.

This, at least, is what Barth attempts in his account of the second word of Ephesians, ἀπόστολος:

> The apostolic vocation splits the person, so to speak. He is an apostle not on the basis of anything he is in and of himself but on the basis of what he is *not*. A demand of a very *different* order is made on him, and a demand of a very different order directs him to his fellow human creatures. There is something exceptional and impossible about him, but it is not his genius, his experience, his unmediated knowledge, or anything that can be accounted for psychologically as greatness or character. What makes him an apostle is his mission, his instructions, and

> the service he is to offer, which are not, from a psychological point of view, even *his own matter* but the matter that *has him* and sends him.[22]

The apostle is defined by the demands laid upon him, by vocation rather than by inherent or even bestowed capacity.[23] The being and act of the ἀπόστολος are wholly a function of Χριστοῦ Ἰησοῦ, both because the apostle is defined by reference to Jesus Christ as the substance of his vocation and because the apostle shares in the paradox of "Immanuel! God with us!"[24] The incarnation is revelation *sub contrario*, in the *coincidentia oppositorum* of God and flesh; and "the existence of an ἀπόστολος is a repetition and variation of the same theme in a subordinate position, where it is possible to serve, to point, and to witness."[25]

Again, reflecting on the phrase "by the will of God" (Eph. 1:1), Barth stresses that apostleship entails abandonment of human privilege and capacity. The divine will "necessarily includes negation in the form of renunciation. Paul renounces all natural protection." The apostle is outside the "composite of well-ordered functions," which we indicate by the term "society." The apostle calls into question the human needs and concerns that cluster around "religion." The apostle gives up "the shelter and protection that he was due by virtue of his human authority," along with "self-honor." In short, the apostle "negates himself."[26]

The denials are forceful and resonant. Their positive intent is to draw attention to the objectivity of apostolic existence and work:

> When [Paul] calls himself ἀπόστολος διὰ θελήματος θεοῦ and addresses his readers on this basis, it is not in order to draw attention to his personal attributes, not even his so-called religious personality, or to flaunt his experience or experiences, or to impress them with his knowledge. He has no reason to linger on these human factors, be they good or evil. His relationship to his readers is determined by his office. He has an objective message to convey, and on the basis of the phrase διὰ θελήματος θεοῦ he appeals to his hearers to receive it objectively.[27]

If there is a weakness here, it is that Barth's eagerness to lift apostleship out of the realm of natural religious personality may inhibit him from speaking not only of the judgment of human nature and powers but also of their sanctification for divine service. In his eagerness to acknowledge the originality of God in relation to the biblical testimony, Barth may at times veer toward a kind of extrinsicism. Yet he also finds that Ephesians presses beyond the antithesis of the divine and the creaturely to speak of their association and of a strange but real human correlate to revelatory divine activity. To this we now turn.

### III

In his exegesis and exposition in these lectures, Barth, we have seen, considers attention to the historical properties of the text to be necessary (in a relatively minimal way) but by no means sufficient for understanding of and intelligent participation in the communicative act of which the apostolic text forms an element. This view of the text and its setting and function in divine revelation is bound up with a set of wider convictions about God and God's relation to creatures, convictions that Barth both takes to the text and finds confirmed by it. They are not given any systematic formulation in the lectures, but they are articulated at various points as he proceeds, sometimes in passing, sometimes more expansively.

As he reads Ephesians, Barth's attention is frequently drawn to the way in which the letter resists any treatment of God as a correlate of human religious or moral culture. Even to speak of God as the object or cause of human knowing, experiencing, and acting is to reduce God to being one term in a pair, folding God into the created reality to which God is related and failing to acknowledge God's entire incommensurability. Commenting, for example, on Ephesians 1:2 ("Grace be with you and peace from God our Father and the Lord Jesus Christ"), Barth stresses that grace and peace are wholly to be understood in terms of God rather than in terms of the subjectivities of believing recipients: "It is *God* we are dealing with here. . . . The realities about which [grace and peace] speak are hidden in *God*, and *God* himself guarantees that they are genuine realities."[28] God himself is

> the incomprehensible *Nevertheless!* at the heart of both terms. . . . When Paul refers to God as the giver of grace and the source of our

> peace, he is not thinking about a conspicuous metaphysical object. When he calls God our "Father," he is using the ultimate parable to express the inexpressible and unimaginable, namely, our origin. *Our* origin: *we* human creatures, although thoroughly human, are related to him, who is most wonderful, who is not and never will be simply a contingent object, who is unknown, who is holy, the *Deus absconditus*.[29]

As often in Barth's early writings, the term "origin" here has a double resonance. In part—as we will see shortly—it indicates the singular character of God's relation to creatures. But it is also a term that Barth uses to reach toward the idea that God is in himself ungrounded, *a se*. In the lectures, Barth has little to say about God's inner life, perfection, and beatitude. Partly this is because he does not find textual prompts to talk about such matters. Partly, again, it may be because what Barth says about God in his writings from this period is still to some degree shaped by the liberal Protestant tradition of which it is sometimes the reverse image; having issued a denial that God is a correlate of human religious life, he does not go on to talk of God's immanent being and acts. When he lectured on Ephesians, Barth had not yet immersed himself in the post-Reformation dogmatics of the inner divine nature and processions, which he was to discover at the prompting of Heinrich Heppe. Moreover, Barth's acute awareness that a theological metaphysics of the divine essence may be a close cousin of idolatry increases his reluctance to make use of such categories in his exposition. For such reasons, rather than talking of God *in se*, Barth usually limits himself to statements about God's relation to creatures, which draw attention to the sheer difference of the *relata* and so to the way in which that relation is unlike any contingent relation, most of all because it is devoid of the mutual presence and exchange that characterize the reciprocal life of creatures. God's relation to creatures is "beyond all relations."[30]

How is this singular relation to be described? A characteristic comment from Barth (he is considering the relation of divine purpose and human approbation in Eph. 1:5–6) runs:

> An infinite qualitative distinction separates the action of the creator from that of the creature. However, this infinite distinction is precisely

> what unites the creature and the creator. God can bless man only as his creature; man can bless God only as his creator. The recognition of this infinite distinction is precisely what makes the blessing and the praise both meet and right. Recognition of God's divinity establishes the divine Otherness, the "*aliter*"; and precisely by being established, it is sublated.[31]

It is important to note that Barth does not think that Ephesians presents either an unrelieved antithesis between or an easy coordination of God and creatures. Rather, as he reads the text, he finds that it compels attention to the acts in which God sets himself before creatures and creatures before himself, on the basis of which their respective natures and the character of their relation in some measure may be perceived.

Barth most commonly describes these acts in the idiom of revelation, understood as the divine act of indirect and interruptive communication, unforeseen and unassimilable, and as an event of manifestation rather than a condition of revealedness. Commenting on "the mystery of [God's] will" in Ephesians 1:9, Barth remarks that the divine will cannot be the object of direct perception "on the basis of what is observable and concrete."[32] He continues: "Because our vision is occluded, an act of revelation is necessary. Every veil must be rent; all human reality must be upended. *God* must speak, and God must *speak*, if we are to understand his will."[33] Immediate knowledge of the will of God is "impossible, even unimaginable for us"; what is vouchsafed to creatures is an event in time, an "incomparable today" in which "time is split" and "the will of God *meets* us."[34] "The *disiecta membra* of this world-reality *do have* a unity. This is so because of *God's* reality, *God's* act, *God's* revelation."[35] The term "revelation" condenses a range of Barth's convictions about the inexhaustibility of God and his unavailability for apprehension on terms other than those in which he presents himself as well as about the instability of creaturely knowledge of God and the impossibility of detached observation or cognitive accumulation and possession.

It is, once again, important to recognize that Barth's demarcations, vigorous and determined though they are, are intended not to deny God's communicative presence but to specify its conditions and the manner of its occurrence. The spiritual blessings of which the apostle speaks in Ephesians 1:3 are not "the presence of God in the form of visible, direct immediacy, which is the domain of gods and idols";[36] they do not simply add to our store of experiential goods. Rather, as the *Spirit's* blessings, they are "God's unmediated presence for us, . . . God in his inapproachability, inaccessibility, and hiddenness. God, who cannot be known, surrounds, besieges, storms, and reorders the domain of my knowing."[37] Spiritual blessings are an event of divine giving, not a given commodity. Again, Barth resists conceptions of a causal relation between God and creatures, which he fears would reduce God to being the first of a series; God is, rather, "beyond the world, beyond all causality."[38] Or again, the relation established by God between himself and creatures must be differentiated from "domesticated piety, which regards *living* with God to be more important than living with *God*."[39] But none of this is intended to negate the relation of God and creatures: the fact that divine presence cannot be made a function of human self-presence "does not obliterate, neutralize, or obviate anything that is mine, positive or negative; but the relativity of all that is mine is clearly revealed, or to be precise, *related* to its origin, measured according to the standard by which all things are decided. . . . What I am, I am in relation to God."[40]

The lectures on Ephesians are an early instance of the way in which, in his theological work in Göttingen, Barth often reaches toward an account of the relation of God and creatures that neither reduces God to a correlate of the human subject nor, by way of correction, simply segregates or opposes God and creatures. In effect, if not in intent, Barth offers a kerygmatically charged appropriation to the scholastic conception of a "mixed" relation between God and creatures—what might be termed an eschatological theological metaphysics of that relation. Properly understood, Barth notes in a comment on Ephesians 1:12, "ἔσχατον . . . refers not only to the last things but also to the first and most important thing in each moment."[41] At this very fertile stage in his development, observes Christopher Asprey,

> Barth's theology . . . proceeds from the conviction that human beings exist before God *eschatologically*. Human ontology is not a settled condition, a "nature" of any kind, but a response to the imposing

> presence of God, who summons me to live beyond myself. What defines this God most fundamentally is not his superiority over all other beings, nor his providential governance of history, but his *encounter* with human beings as their *God*. Both aspects are indispensable: God is not conceived in abstraction from his creation, yet he meets it in such commanding superiority that, just as importantly, *it* may not extract itself from *him*. This encounter is what is meant by revelation.[42]

A closely similar pattern of thought is evident in Barth's christological remarks in the lectures. At the opening of the letter, the author speaks of himself as ἀπόστολος Χριστοῦ Ἰησοῦ; and "Jesus Christ"—a proper name set together with an office of universal scope—"means the unification of all that is inherently incompatible, the *coincidentia oppositorum*, and the complete riddle of Christology."[43] Incarnation does not mean peaceful coordination of divine and human natures: in Christ, opposites coincide but remain opposites (an early expression from Barth of the instinct behind the *extra Calvinisticum*, perhaps). Further, the reality that the name indicates does not present itself as a matter for calm contemplation. It is an assault: "the message of the incarnation is not proclaimed as an idea . . . ; rather, the word from the peaceful kingdom enters the world as a battle cry, as a declaration of war. Here, the δύναμις τοῦ θεοῦ speaks. Here, the One God demands an acknowledgment. . . . Here, the One God determines to rule as monarch, and *all* other demands with which life confronts us are called into question by him. Here, it is a matter of God's decisive battle against idols."[44] The very humanity in which revelation takes form subverts any attempt to integrate it into an existing experience or scheme: "in order to . . . prevent us from turning it into a religious or philosophical truth, to impress upon us that the truth comes to us only in the eternal moment of knowledge, the concrete subject matter of this gospel and its most characteristic trait is a human face, the completely mysterious face of one who suffers, is rejected, and dies—the face of Jesus of Nazareth, who was crucified."[45] Yet this is not a disavowal of God's presence in Christ but an attempt to spell out its origin and its distinctive properties. "'Ἐν Χριστῷ means Immanuel! God with us! Ἐν Χριστῷ God draws near in his self-revelation, while remaining distant, strange, and incomprehensible: the *Deus absconditus*. In Christ is thus *the* proximity of God, which always means eternity and never merely the temporal extension of what is palpable, comprehensible, or perceptible. Precisely because the proximity of God is ultimate reality, it can only be believed—and the belief itself is the wonder of its revelation."[46] Because in Christ divine revelation is asymptotic, it breaks the assumption, which Barth found to be deep-seated in the exegesis, dogmatics, and ethics of the liberal Protestant tradition, that the real is the historical-experiential.

God is beyond—not constituted by—all relations; nevertheless, he sets himself before creatures and brings them into relation to himself. In what ways does this relation take creaturely form?

Barth is markedly reluctant to say much about how objective relation to God coincides with creaturely subjectivity, because he is recoiling from theologies in which religious subjectivity enjoys priority. Commenting on "sealed with the Holy Spirit of promise" (Eph. 1:13), for example, he does not take the occasion to speak of the Spirit as the agent of the realization of divine benefits in the believer, and he emphasizes contingency rather than appropriation:

> Humanity and everything human is questionable. What is not in question is the relation of humanity and everything human to *God*. The more we recognize humanity's uncertainty, the more we recognize the certainty of man's relation to God. Indeed, the reason human existence in and of itself is dubious is precisely because humanity is originally related to God. Everything that is contingent and temporal is relative. What is not relative is the actual relation to the *Absolute*. The more clearly we recognize this relation for what it is, the more clearly we understand the relativity of all things."[47]

Because contingency is by far the most important attribute of creaturely relation to God, the creatures of divine grace are defined not by divinely given powers to act or dispositions or forms of life and experience but by reference to their origin in God, the counterpart to which is a lack of creaturely extension.

What, Barth asks in his lecture on Ephesians 1:7, does it mean that we "have" (ἔχομεν) redemption and other divine blessings? In considering this "having," we are not to think that "our feet touch the familiar ground of human being, having, and doing, where we can catch our breath for a moment," for here "our familiar human being, having, and doing are called into question from beyond."[48] Our having is not possession but rather the (unfinishable) process of coming to have, incessant reception. "We have what only God has, what we [can] have only in God, who unites time and eternity. In other words, we have what we must receive continuously from God in each present moment."[49] This triggers some critical remarks on the "Biblical Realism" of J. T. Beck; though Barth had learned from Beck's unease with critical theology in the school of F. C. Baur and had made use of Beck's work on Ephesians,[50] he is troubled by the way in which Beck's "realism" drifts into a noneschatological subjectivism. Beck's concern to go beyond the extrinsicism of some Protestant theologies of justification and speak of the intrinsic reality of divine grace threatens to become "simply a form of naturalism."[51] "The Word of God does not become more real by being refashioned into human reality. We should be content with its own reality rather than trying to make it conform to ours."[52]

An important corollary here is that the creature's relation to God does not follow an ordered temporal course; it is not discursive but always at the beginning. The knowledge with which the apostle (in Eph. 1:15–23) asks that his recipients be blessed is—precisely as "the blessing of *God*"—"completely new each new moment,"[53] a constantly renewed divine act of giving, such that "we must return continually to the source and origin. This origin does not exist in the world or within time," and so "the human creature must repeatedly *call upon* God as God."[54] As often in his earlier (and sometimes in his later) writing, Barth makes much of the idea of newness in order to emphasize that life in relation to God is not an amplification of natural being in time, for God's action is punctiliar, not durative. "Any truth that is *not new* does not qualify as God's truth. Likewise, when redemption ceases to be an object of hope and becomes something we possess or consume, it is no longer redemption."[55] "If we regard [God's] name, kingdom, and will as no more than the evolution, extension, or continuation of what already exists—then obviously we do not know what we are saying when we say 'God.'"[56] Relation to God is marked above all not by the accumulation and enjoyment of spiritual goods but by prayer for fresh acts of grace:

"A new day has dawned. Yesterday's discovery must be sought anew today."[57]

Similar patterns of thought recur throughout Barth's comments on Christian existence in the course of the lectures. Early on, he considers the apostle's designation of his recipients as τοῖς ἁγίοις τοῖς οὖσιν . . . καὶ πιστοῖς ἐν Χριστῷ Ἰησοῦ (Eph. 1:1). Neither holiness nor faithfulness may on Barth's reckoning be understood as modifications of human subjectivity in time: "Ἅγιος signifies a place, object, or person, which, although situated in the known world, belongs not to this world but to the rule of God's power and splendor";[58] it thus indicates "a *negation*, a cordoning off, the imposition of a blockade, an attack that creates a void, like the crater formed from an exploding shell."[59] Moreover, both its cause and its effects are unavailable for direct perception. "The one who makes them holy . . . does not appear as such, occupying time and space. . . . There is no way to directly identify the state of holiness as such! Holiness that is conspicuous, tangible, or perceptible (humanly speaking) is not holiness."[60] And so Barth once again counters what he regards as a deleterious historical stability by insisting on the interruptive, occasional character of God's relation to the creature and the irregularity of its creaturely complement. "Holiness," he writes,

> is a relationship with *God*. This relationship is established by *God*. It is never simply a given. It is never a finished event. For the human creature, it will always remain a quest and goal; but as free grace, it becomes more than a quest and goal. It exists wonderfully, moment by moment, on the basis of God's eternal election; and absolutely *no* law could possibly be at work, above or apart from God's *beneplacitum*, diverting the course of this election. To *call a person holy* is to say that God eternally disturbs him and fills him with joy, that God has laid his hand upon the creature. The creature is attacked and wounded where he is most vital, in his subjectivity, his existence. Existentially, he is no longer his own. He himself no longer lives. He resembles an off-centered wheel, which no longer revolves around its own center.[61]

Moreover, the action and presence of God are entirely invisible and generate no creaturely form: "all we can see is the creature, living in sin and death."[62] Yet, crucially for Barth, the absence of historical form or visibility betokens not divine absence but simply the mode of God's relation to the creature: "unlike all gods and idols, he draws near while maintaining his infinite distance."[63] Because of this, *malgré tout*, we may say that there is a human reality of holiness, that "in Christ, the human creature is sanctified."[64] Such holiness is real not as an "experience" or "condition"[65] but because of its divine basis, which Barth describes as "the human creature's *eternal* relation to God, *the* relation in which the person *is* eternal and will become what he certainly never was and *becomes* what he eternally is: God's possession, instrument, servant, and child. This relation is real only because it begins where *everything* comes to an end, in *the* life that comes from death."[66]

Similarly, reflecting on the description of the recipients of the letter as πιστοῖς, Barth steers away from any correlation of God and creatures. "The idea of polarity, equipoise, or balance between divine and human action is absent from Paul's thought; wherever 'faith' is spoken of in such a fashion, it leads to simplistic and false dogmatics."[67] Barth admits that πιστοῖς does in some way refer "to a truly subjective human state,"[68] but the concession is immediately qualified:

> Faith is the action of the new person in me, the person *I am not*, the new person whose identity within me is the source of the greatest possible honor. Faith is a fundamental and eternal event that is beyond all temporal processes. Faith is God's work in us. It takes place in us, to be sure; it is not some invisible metaphysical reality, independent of our recognition of God's mercy, enclosed in his holiness. But it takes place only as God's work, as the eternal moment hidden within the temporal moment; it is one with what occurs in us.[69]

## IV

It would be relatively easy to judge Barth's lectures, both in what they say about divine revelation and its apostolic media and in their presentation of Christian existence in relation to God, as often trapped by the malign contrast: *aut gloria Dei aut gloria hominis*. Such an opposition is not Barth's intention: the lectures (along with those on Calvin from the following semester) are in part a struggle to articulate a relation between the "vertical" and the "horizontal" that is neither antithesis nor synthesis. So intense is Barth's concern to draw attention to the nongiven, nonrepresentable character of God's presence that he allows himself to say rather little about the human forms and acts by which divine revelation and saving action are communicated and received and about the ways in which they shape and order human life and activity—beyond some highly charged descriptions of the dislocation that they engender. Together with Barth's instinctive occasionalism and his insistent rhetoric, this intensity runs the risk of denying what, after many qualifications, he is trying to affirm. In the *Church Dogmatics*, Barth will leave this difficulty behind in his long descriptions of God's economic acts and the human moral history that they evoke and sustain. Here, however, his principal concern is to refuse to think of God and creatures as reciprocal, commensurable terms; yet in so doing, he sometimes appears to subvert not only commensurability but all relation.

What Barth is reaching toward in his exegesis and exposition is an understanding of God and creatures in which, because God is perfect, simple, and uncompounded, God's relation to creatures is not constitutive of his being. The protest against any settled forms of creaturely relation to God are directed against the idea that God is merely one *res* alongside another. To issue the protest, Barth often appeals to one or another element of the theology of divine grace; but grace is identified primarily with divine freedom rather than with the communication of goods or with an ever-fresh act of divine giving rather than with its creaturely effects. An account of the matter less concerned to voice dissent might make its appeal to divine goodness—to the beneficence that flows from God's fullness of life and that enacts his purpose to cause, sustain, and bless creaturely life in its integrity and continuity. Yet there is a reminder in what Barth struggled to articulate to his audience almost a century ago: only when we have come to know that God is beyond all relations may we understand and enact the relation to him in which we have been caused to stand.

# Exposition of Ephesians

Winter Semester 1921–22

KARL BARTH

Epheserbrief

W. S. 1921/22

1, 1–2

10. XI. 21

KBA 1664. 1

Page one of the handwritten manuscript of Barth's first Ephesians lecture of Winter Semester 1921–22, on Ephesians 1:1–2. The lecture is dated November 10, 1921.

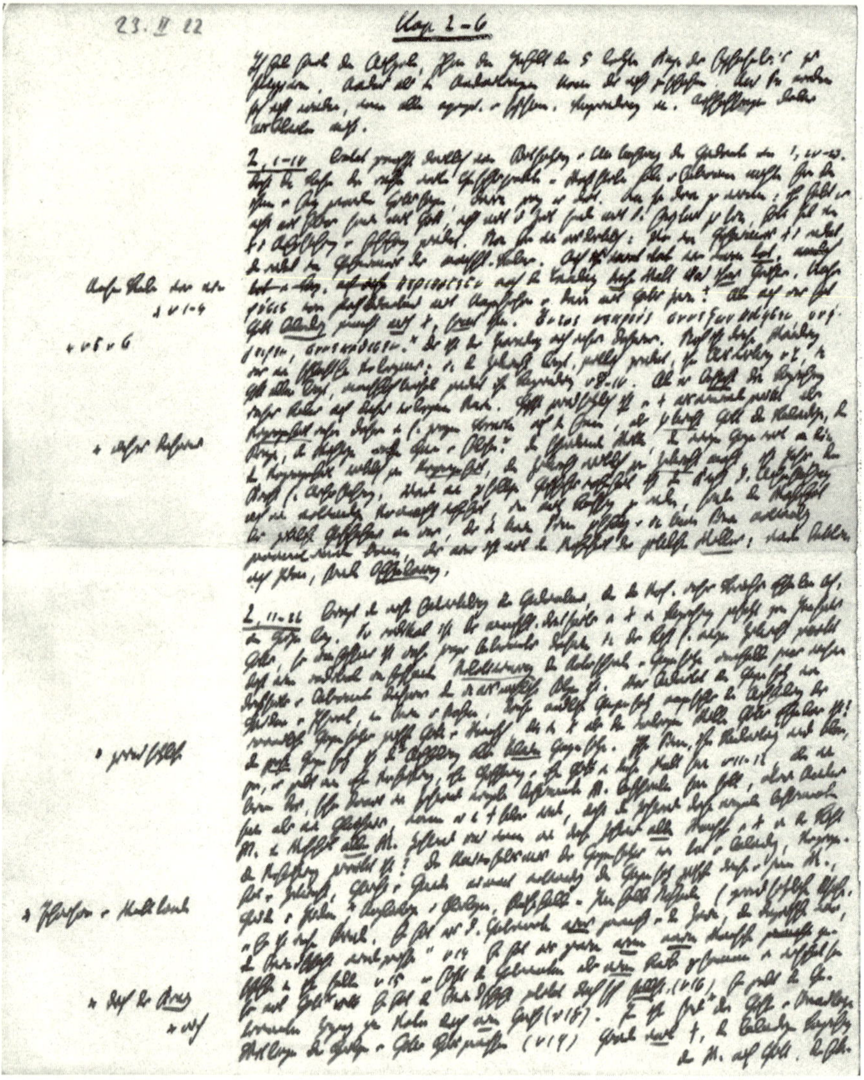

Page one of the handwritten manuscript of Barth's final Ephesians lecture of Winter Semester 1921–22, a summary of Ephesians 2–6. The lecture is dated February 23, 1922. (Photos courtesy of the Karl Barth-Archiv.)

# Ephesians 1:1–2

*Nov. 10, 1921*

[[1] Παῦλος ἀπόστολος Χριστοῦ Ἰησοῦ διὰ θελήματος θεοῦ τοῖς ἁγίοις τοῖς οὖσιν [ἐν Ἐφέσῳ] καὶ πιστοῖς ἐν Χριστῷ Ἰησοῦ, [2] χάρις ὑμῖν καὶ εἰρήνη ἀπὸ θεοῦ πατρὸς ἡμῶν καὶ κυρίου Ἰησοῦ Χριστοῦ.]

*[1] Paul, an apostle of Christ Jesus by the will of God, to the saints and believers in Christ Jesus. [2] Grace be with you and peace from God our Father and the Lord Jesus Christ.*

Ephesians 1:1–2 is the letter's "preface" and consists of an identification and brief description of the author of the letter and its recipients.

Παῦλος. The first word of our epistle has attracted more attention and certainly more interest than all the other words in the letter put together during the era of historical-critical research of the Bible, which has certainly not yet run its course. The question is raised whether the apostle Paul is actually the author of the epistle or whether an unknown student of Paul placed the famous man's name on his own work, a perfectly acceptable practice at the time. In contrast to the unanimity that still existed less than thirty years ago, when one camp of New Testament scholarship prevailed, the current consensus on the matter can be summarized as a cautious *non liquet*[1] within which individual scholars defend a position, with more or less certainty, for or against the letter's authenticity. The excursus that

Martin Dibelius provides in his discussion of verse 4:16 reflects the current state of the debate.[2] In addition to that discussion, I refer you to the clear accounts of the matter in the New Testament introductions by Adolf Jülicher[3] and by Fritz Barth;[4] and because I am not in a position to take up the cudgels in the controversy, which seems to have abated recently, I will limit myself to briefly identifying the main points in order to explain my own position on the matter, which is in no way original. The debate, if I am correct, can be reduced to two central points.

The first point concerns the *close relationship between Ephesians and Colossians* at the level of both vocabulary and ideas. Undoubtedly, this relationship is not merely accidental, as even a superficial comparison of the two letters reveals. It follows that if both letters are genuine, they belong to the same period of Paul's life as Philippians, that is, the time of his Roman imprisonment. They form a closely related group and must be interpreted by continuously examining the parallel passages so that one serves as a commentary on the other. Now, it is claimed that because Ephesians appears to be dependent on Colossians, it could not possibly have been written by someone with a mind like Paul's, but is the product of a redactor, who was a disciple of Paul. And because Colossians is shorter and its historical setting more certain, it has tended to overshadow Ephesians, which tends to be regarded with a certain suspicion or as less valuable. The decisive evidence against this view, in my opinion, is the impossibility of interpreting the alleged redactor without recourse to suspiciously complicated hypotheses, such as those advocated by Henrich Holtzmann.[5] Nothing is ruled out, resulting in an arbitrary configuring of the parallel passages, not to mention tendentiousness in the passages selected. It seems to me much more likely that *one* author wrote both letters, drawing from the same conceptual framework but expressing his ideas in different situations, freely adapting his own ideas the second time, repeating, paraphrasing, and occasionally modifying them, much as any of us might do today when we have lectured on or written about similar material to different audiences.[6] The occasional use of the same term to express different ideas, a matter on which Dibelius places such great weight and which he demonstrates in reference to the terms σῶμα and μυστήριον, for example,[7] does not seem to me to be sufficient evidence to refute this view, considering the extreme dialectical flexibility that Paul usually displays (for example, in his use of the term νόμος within Romans alone).

The second point is more difficult. It concerns the peculiar *linguistic and conceptual material* that is characteristic of Ephesians (some of which also appears in Philippians and Colossians and some of which is unique to Ephesians), compared to Paul's so-called major letters. We must first examine the facts of the matter and then assess their significance. And in fact, if we come to Ephesians after reading the Corinthian correspondence, for example,[8] we find material that differs in both style and content from the undisputed letters, while many of the normal Pauline features are conspicuously absent. In the very first paragraph (1:3–14), we encounter a variety of unusual terms, such as τὰ ἐπουράνια, καταβολὴ κόσμου, χαριτοῦν, and προελπίζειν; and in the same place, we are confronted with a sentence construction so convoluted that it is difficult to understand, let alone reflect upon. Closer scrutiny reveals a variety of curious gems in the same unusual, embellished, and ceremonial style (it has been called "solemn")[9], which is so characteristic of Ephesians; whereas we look in vain for the familiar, signature Pauline terms, such as δικαιοῦν, θάνατος, θέλειν, and φρονεῖν, just to name a few, as well as the short exclamatory phrases, such as τί οὖν and μὴ γένοιτο, and the edgy, agitated, and explicitly polemical style that we find in Romans and Galatians.

More importantly, we are confronted with significant material differences between Ephesians and the undisputed letters. Here, Christ is exalted to such a position or rank that interpreters describe recourse to the phrase "cosmic Christ"[10] or to "metaphysical" language.[11] Here, in curious juxtaposition with this so-called cosmic Christ, the theme of the church suddenly appears right at the center of things. Here, we catch a glimpse into the realm of good and evil spirits. Here, we see all of Christendom from the vantage point of the *mystery*, μυστήριον, which was long concealed but is now revealed, and thus in light of the characteristics of God, on the one hand, and the human characteristics necessary for salvation, on the other—the intellectual properties, the gnosis, which is related to them but exists on a higher plane.[12] Here, in several passages the apostles are ranked with the prophets as historical personages, imbued with holiness—a particularly difficult point. Here, the great battle over the *validity of the law* has receded into the distance, now sounding like the rumbling of distant thunder. And where is the *parousia expectation*, which figures so prominently in Paul's early epistles? Here, the church seems to attain perfection through a kind of natural evolution, without even a hint that a catastrophe of any kind is necessary to bring about its perfection.[13] There is, to quote Holtzmann, "the notion of an assured and inexorable surging movement, which proceeds from Christ's imbuing everything with the effects of his immanence."[14]

Nevertheless, we should not overestimate the significance of these differences. They are striking but not unprecedented. The modified style that Paul uses here is understandable, given his new train of thought. Both his altered mode of expression and the partially new ideas can be explained by the letter's different provenance, compared to the major letters. Ephesians is the product of the elderly Paul.[15] I hope that you will not take this as a criticism, but if we consider the peculiar directions that, in their later years, Plato,[16] Schelling,[17] or even a contemporary like Paul Natorp[18] developed their ideas, both formally and materially, we have a plausible analogy to the relationship of Ephesians to, say, Romans. There was truly a more astonishing evolution than we normally attribute to Paul if he was in fact the author of Ephesians. Even the scholars who currently regard the letter as unauthentic acknowledge that most of its vocabulary and contents is clearly Pauline.[19] How we evaluate many of the things that at first glance strike us as either anomalous or conspicuously absent (here I am thinking expressly about parousia expectation) depends on the degree to which the reader or scholar is able to interpret dialectically and therefore not be thrown off course but to follow the thread from here to there and to discover the new in the old and rediscover the old in the new. How easily someone in a later century could mistake one of Natorp's authentic writings as unauthentic. Such a mistake is possible if one merely reads the words and clinically establishes what is there rather than following the text and thinking along with it as it stands. Regrettably, even Holtzmann, such a profitable scholar in other respects, is slightly ponderous in this regard.

Personally, I would defend the authenticity of Ephesians. But frankly, I do not have any great interest in the question. As far as

I am concerned, it could be otherwise. I have treated the matter this thoroughly in order to fulfill all righteousness (cf. Matt. 3:15). Bengel expresses my true opinion about it when he says, "*Noli quaerere quis scripserit sed quid scriptum est.*"[20] Now that we have behind us this unavoidable matter of New Testament introduction, we can happily devote ourselves entirely to "*quod scriptum est.*" As for the authorship question, it is enough to know that someone, at any rate, wrote Ephesians (why not Paul?) thirty to sixty years after Christ's death (hardly any later than that, since it is attested by Ignatius, Polycarp, and Justin),[21] someone who understood Paul well and developed the apostle's ideas with obvious loyalty as well as originality.

Ἀπόστολος, the author of the epistle calls himself. The literal meaning of ἀπόστολος is "ambassador." Surprisingly, in classical Greek it was a technical term for "admiral," according to Hans Lietzmann's discussion of Romans 1:1.[22] And even if this meaning of the word is not directly attested in the New Testament, we can certainly assume that at one time it had a military ring, which it no longer has for us. In the New Testament, initially only the twelve disciples were called "apostles." Then Paul assumed the title, claiming God as his sole authority. It was used more generally for a while. Barnabas is so designated in Acts 14:4, 14. Second Corinthians 8:23 refers to so-called ἀπόστολοι ἐκκλησιῶν. Ψευδαπόστολοι also crop up (2 Cor. 11:13; Rev. 2:2). In the *Didache* and the *Shepherd of Hermas*, ἀπόστολος seems to be almost a synonym for "preacher."[23] Later, this general use is discontinued, and once more it is used as a designation of honor for the Twelve, including Paul.[24] An apostle is a person with a mission and the power to carry it out. He is sent to enemy-occupied territory to break up a blockade, so to speak. We should think about the ἀπόστολοι as the messengers of the βασιλεία, of the royal rule. Certainly, no one is an ἀπόστολος by virtue of being a preacher—or anything else, for that matter, not even the greatest poet, thinker, or artist. As Kierkegaard says, "The vocation of apostle is a paradoxical fact" (*Über den Unterschied zwischen einem Apostel und einem Genie*).[25] The apostolic vocation splits the person, so to speak. He is an apostle not on the basis of anything he is in and of himself but on the basis of what he is *not*. A demand of a very *different* order is made on him, and a demand of a very different order directs him to his fellow human creatures. There is something exceptional and impossible about him, but it is not his genius, his experience, his unmediated knowledge,[26] or anything that can be accounted for psychologically as greatness or character. What makes him an apostle is his mission, his instructions, and the service he is to offer, which are not, from a psychological point of view, even *his own matter*[27] but the matter that *has him* and sends him. That is the source of his burden [*Bürde*], and that is the source of his honor [*Würde*]. The order to which he submits imposes a limit, not only on himself but also on anything that might harm him, rendering him intrepid, secure, and unshakable, once and for all.

Ἀπόστολος Χριστοῦ Ἰησοῦ, Paul calls himself and thereby indicates the source of his authority.[28] This phrase, Χριστὸς Ἰησοῦς, Christ Jesus, or with the reverse emphasis, Jesus, the Christ, contains and reveals the essence of Paul's teaching—and not only Paul's. Time does not permit a thorough discussion of the phrase here, and I can only briefly suggest its meaning. As you know, in this context Χριστός, "Messiah," means "the anointed king of Israel," an eminent historical figure from the bright but distant past who now personifies the eschatological expectation. He is the one from above, who brings and restores the kingdom. All of that is easy for us to say, but what an upheaval of heaven and earth must have occurred in the late Jewish period to generate such an expectation and such a concept! And how astonishing that when the gospel of Israel's Christ was directed to the whole world, it displaced so many other rival claims at the time and met with such success! Most of all, how incomprehensible is the actual content of this gospel! An individual, particular, and historical man, Jesus of Nazareth, *is* this Χριστός. He is the κύριος, the Lord, to use the term that was common in both political and religious language of the period. *A* man is *the* man. All others are shadows of him. As they wait expectantly for him, they wait for their own fulfillment. The phrase Χριστὸς Ἰησοῦς means the unification of all that is inherently incompatible, the *coincidentia oppositorum*,[29] and the complete riddle of Christology over which later centuries labored. But what are we saying? This phrase, Χριστὸς Ἰησοῦς, speaks to the most profound problem of life that confronts all of us. Is not your life in time, and mine, this particular, random, unique existence of ours, included in the demand that we *should* share as well as the promise that we *may* share in the source of ultimate truth and reality; not only partially, or spiritually, but down to the last detail; not only as parts of a whole but as a whole; not only as the member of a group but as an individual?

Moreover, the form of this announcement is determined by its content. Note well: "Christ" or "Messiah" means "king." There is an unmistakable progression from king to ἀπόστολος, to envoys who are instructed and equipped with power. The message of the incarnation is not proclaimed as an idea, in the normal sense of the word; rather, the word from the peaceful kingdom enters the world as a battle cry, as a declaration of war. Here, the δύναμις τοῦ θεοῦ speaks.[30] Here, the One God demands an acknowledgment, which initially is not acknowledged, then *is* acknowledged. Here, the One God determines to rule as monarch, and *all* other demands with which life confronts us are called into question by him. Here, it is a matter of God's decisive battle against idols. And in order to assure that we take this battle seriously, to prevent us from turning it into a religious or philosophical truth, to impress upon us that the truth comes to us only in the eternal moment of knowledge, the concrete subject matter of this gospel and its most characteristic trait is a human face, the completely mysterious face of one who suffers, is rejected, and dies—the face of Jesus of Nazareth, who was crucified. Obviously, the office of ἀπόστολος must be understood as a parable. As with the master, so it is with the disciples. Paradox can be explained only through paradox. Immanuel! God with us [Matt. 1:23]! That is the meaning of the phrase Χριστὸς Ἰησοῦς. The existence of an ἀπόστολος is a repetition and variation of the same theme in a subordinate position, where it is possible to serve, to point, and to witness. To be an ἀπόστολος means to serve Χριστὸς Ἰησοῦς. But he can *only* serve him. To be Christ himself is out of the question. Think about the meaning of the pastoral vocation to which you aspire. The pastoral office has meaning only because of the existence of the apostolic office. And the actual theme of this office is that the unheard of event has become a reality in Christ. Consequently, it is a matter of serving in that office where one can *only* serve.

Paul adds, διὰ θελήματος θεοῦ, exactly the same phrase as in 1 Corinthians 1:1; 2 Corinthians 1:1; Colossians 1:1; 2 Timothy 1:1; and expressed more clearly and precisely in Galatians 1:1: οὐκ ἀπ' ἀνθρώπων οὐδὲ δι' ἀνθρώπου ἀλλὰ διὰ Ἰησοῦ Χριστοῦ καὶ θεοῦ πατρὸς τοῦ ἐγείραντος αὐτὸν ἐκ νεκρῶν. The will of God is what makes an apostle to be an apostle. This will of God is identified in the Galatians passage as the same incomprehensible will that awakened Jesus from the dead. For this reason, it necessarily includes negation in the form of renunciation. Paul renounces all natural protection. He abandons all the normal defenses that he or anyone might take advantage of. Anyone who risks saying what Paul had to say inevitably becomes open to the accusation of being *presumptuous*. Human society has always been, in principle if not in practice, a composite of well-ordered functions, which are recognized (more or less) as necessary and useful—as the organization of a university, for example, reveals on a small scale. But what gives a person the right to speak about *God* and about the last things? How does one justify the necessity and the usefulness of *this* function? We can appeal to people's "religious" needs, of course. Such a human foundation for the apostolic office is, as we all know, the safeguard and defense that the church has always enjoyed in the fabric of human society. In that case, speaking about God is considered a *legitima vocatio*. This human basis for the apostolic office obviously played an important role even in primitive Christianity. Its definitive development occurred in the Roman Catholic Church, and analogous developments can be observed in all other religions. Basically, the idea is unobjectionable. How could religion not, either tacitly or explicitly, conform to the rules that govern all human affairs?

But what if someone has something to say that transcends "religion" and all recognized human needs and concerns so profoundly that it radically calls them into question, along with the fabric of society that is based upon them? What authorizes a Socrates, a Paul, or a Kierkegaard? Is it not obvious that people like this leave themselves open to the accusation that they are presumptuous or that they are enthusiasts or nihilists when they prefer not to cover up the facts, even as they seek accommodations within the shaky construction of human activities along with everyone else? Paul preferred not to cover up the facts. He never did so with the apostles, just as they never disguised *their* churchly authority. He renounces the shelter and protection that he was due by virtue of his human authority. With his appeal to διὰ θελήματος, he risks being taken for a fool, and that is precisely what happened. He will not assume any authority that is not granted to him by God. In this light perhaps his God-given authority is best understood as *humility*. He renounces self-honor precisely because he seeks honor from God alone. Most of all, by appealing to this διὰ θελήματος θεοῦ, he negates himself. Receiving honor from others is surely the subtlest form of attributing honor to ourselves. And because he is basically not afraid of offending anyone with his claim, he has become impervious to the accusation of being presumptuous. In the case of the apostolic vocation, no one except God and God alone can say to a person, "You are [an apostle], not an enthusiast!" Consequently, he must accept the humiliation that may be laid upon him, and in most cases *is* laid upon him, because he can do no other.*

*Nov. 17, 1921*

The phrase ἀπόστολος διὰ θελήματος θεοῦ is dialectical: it has two different meanings that are contradictory but at the same time define each other and therefore point beyond themselves. The meaning of the phrase is found in *that to which they point*. Is it supreme self-confidence or profound humility that Paul demonstrates here? Is the cause of Paul's supreme self-confidence precisely that humility with which he refuses to claim any human appointment, appealing

*Barth deleted the following paragraph but incorporated the contents, worded slightly differently, in his second lecture, delivered on November 17:

> Last time we ended with the Pauline phrase διὰ θελήματος θεοῦ and established that with this expression the author consciously both opens himself to *and* frees himself from the reproach of presumptuousness. It is an expression of his self-confidence *and* his humility. If his honor as ἀπόστολος were established through people, even the best people, this apparent humility would actually be arrogance for him, a form of seeking his own, human honor. By appealing to the will of God, this apparent arrogance is actually humility for him, because by it he renounces all that is considered valuable by people. The visible manifestation of this expression is that the writer becomes neutral and indifferent.

instead to the fact that God has appointed him? Or is it the other way around? Is true apostolic humility precisely what gives him the self-confidence to lower his guard? Can we really say conclusively that it is either one or the other?

When arrogance is humility and humility arrogance, then clearly there is another factor at work. We need to gain a wider vantage point where self-confidence and humility are equally appropriate and even necessary. Paul is referring to the sphere where the word seizes us, neutralizing and bypassing both our *exemplary behavior* and our bad habits, that which is *commendable* as well as that which is reprehensible about us. When he calls himself ἀπόστολος διὰ θελήματος θεοῦ and addresses his readers on this basis, it is not in order to draw attention to his personal attributes, not even his so-called religious personality, or to flaunt his experience or experiences,[31] or to impress them with his knowledge. He has no reason to linger on these human factors, be they good or evil. His relationship to his readers is determined by his office. He has an objective message to convey, and on the basis of the phrase διὰ θελήματος θεοῦ he appeals to his hearers to receive it objectively. Listen to what Calvin has to say about this passage in a sermon delivered on May 15, 1558:

> For one of the common artifices which the devil uses to diminish reverence for God's Word is to place before our eyes the person who brings it. Now it is certain that we are frail vessels and of no value, yes, of no more worth than broken pots. What is there in those whom God has ordained to be the ministers of his Word? But the treasure is inestimably great at all times, despite the contemptibleness of the vessels [2 Cor. 4:7]. Let us take note then that when men come to bear testimony to the forgiveness of our sins and the salvation we ought to hope for, our faith must rise up higher and not stand questioning whether such a man is worthy to be heard or not, or enquiring what manner of person he is. Let us content ourselves with the thought that God by that means intends to draw us to himself.[32]

A *true* bearer of the divine word would not dare disqualify himself by preaching another gospel (1 Cor. 9:27). He, most of all, stands under the purifying judgment of this word. Certainly his human nature, what we tend to refer to as his "personality," including his religious personality, is affected by this purifying judgment. How could it be otherwise? But what is purified and refashioned by the word remains *human*; and this refashioning and cleansing take place through *judgment*, the repeated judgment of the word. The human creature is a mortal bearer of that word. Remembering this judgment prevents the bearer of the word from confusing *God's* questions and answers with any other theme, with his own being, having, and doing—even his supremely religious being, having, and doing. This recollection should also prevent his hearers or readers from becoming preoccupied with the messenger instead of the message. "For our boast is this, the testimony of our conscience" (2 Cor. 1:12). However, "We do not preach ourselves, but Christ Jesus as Lord, and ourselves as your servants for Jesus' sake" (2 Cor. 4:5).

We now turn to the description of the letter's *recipients*, whom Paul describes as τοῖς ἁγίοις . . . καὶ πιστοῖς ἐν Χριστῷ Ἰησοῦ. The words τοῖς οὖσιν (and subsequently ἐν Ἐφέσῳ) were added later.

Ἅγιοι is first, both in sequence and in order of importance (as in Col. 1:2). Paul does not use the phrase ἁγίοις . . . καὶ πιστοῖς to describe his readers in Galatians or 1 and 2 Thessalonians, referring to them simply as ἐκκλησία θεοῦ (or ἐκκλησίαι θεοῦ, Gal. [1:2]). It is only in Romans 1:7; 1 Corinthians 1:2, 2 Corinthians 1:1; and Philippians 1:1 that he uses the term ἅγιοι. The addition of πιστοί, here and in Colossians 1:2, is distinctive of the mature style of Paul's later epistles, in which he develops concepts more fully. In these salutations πιστοί never occurs without ἅγιοι. This fact alone tells us that ἅγιοι is the more important term: it is not defined by πιστοί; rather, πιστοί must be understood in light of ἅγιοι.

In the Old Testament, which is clearly the background for Paul's use of the term here, ἅγιος signifies a place, object, or person, which, although situated in the known world, belongs not to this world but to the rule of God's power and splendor. Therefore, ἅγιος describes a *negation*, a cordoning off, the imposition of a blockade, an attack that creates a void, like the crater formed from an exploding shell.[33] This negation is strictly *paradoxical*. By creaturely standards of thinking and experience, the person or thing that is hallowed remains unchanged. The one who makes them holy, the cause of this negation, does not appear as such, occupying time and space.

The sanction, the demands, and the threat that this event introduces cannot be perceived; neither can the void that occurs in a creaturely object or a person and by virtue of which they are what they really are not. Strictly speaking, ἅγιος means that $a = (-a)$. Only God can guarantee that this determination is *divine* and therefore real. There is no way to directly identify the state of holiness as such! Holiness that is conspicuous, tangible, or perceptible (humanly speaking) is not holiness. Apart from God, nothing is holy by virtue of what it is or is not in and of itself. None of us is holy by virtue of what we believe or do not believe, by what we do or do not do. God is the one who makes holy what will always remain unholy. And *God* reveals what is holy as he makes the creature holy. Only the holy *of God* exist in the sphere where *God himself* is holy and has plans for them that they cannot thwart; any holiness based on human effort would be our own rather than the holiness that is uniquely and completely God's.

Holiness is a relationship with *God*. This relationship is established by *God*. It is never simply a given. It is never a finished event. For the human creature, it will always remain a quest and goal; but as free grace, it becomes more than a quest and goal. It exists wonderfully, moment by moment, on the basis of God's eternal election; and absolutely *no* law could possibly be at work, above or apart from God's *beneplacitum*,[34] diverting the course of this election. To *call a person holy* is to say that God eternally disturbs him and fills him with joy, that God has laid his hand upon the creature. The creature is attacked and wounded where he is most vital, in his subjectivity, his existence. Existentially, he is no longer his own. He himself no longer lives. He resembles an off-centered wheel, which no longer revolves around its own center. As God first appeared to Abraham (cf. Gen. 18:1–15), God appears at his dwelling like a stranger, making promises and demanding obedience. Has a miracle occurred? No, there is no miracle. Everywhere we turn, all we can see is the creature, living in sin and death. God remains hidden—fundamentally hidden—after he has revealed himself to the creature. Precisely because he has wrapped himself in the impenetrable mystery of his divinity, he has revealed himself as *the creature's God*: as *the creature's* God because he is infinitely near those who are utterly lost, destitute, and lonely, whose gods and idols lie shattered before them. But he has also revealed himself as the creature's *God* because unlike all gods and idols, he draws near while maintaining his infinite distance; in sovereign freedom, he draws near the creature while remaining utterly unapproachable. When God claims a person as his holy one, what occurs is not a miracle but a wonder, the wonder of the act of knowing.[35]

Ἐν Χριστῷ Ἰησοῦ, which follows πιστοί, refers first and foremost to ἅγιοι. In Christ, the human creature is sanctified (Eph. 5:25–26; 1 Cor. 1:2; Gal. 1:4; Col. 1:22). Remember what we said about Christ in the previous lecture. Christ is the claim that God makes on a person, the hand laid upon him, the ultimatum addressed to him, God's declaration that this sinful, mortal creature belongs to the jurisdiction of God's authority and glory. In this context, the Old Testament claim that our God is a consuming fire takes on new significance (cf. Exod. 24:17; Deut. 4:24; 9:3; Heb. 12:29). Christ is the place in which the question about God becomes so acute that it must be simultaneously God's answer. Here, everything appears to be a riddle from the human point of view; therefore, precisely here we find the divine solution to all riddles. Here God's holiness speaks the final, shattering word—mercy. In Christ, the human creature in all of his spectacular incompetence is a holy person—he is holy as his God is holy. I am speaking about Christ, crucified and risen, as Paul did, not about the pious man Jesus or about a psychological relationship between us and this pious man, a path that leads somehow from him to us or some particular experience that we could have of him. Paul certainly did not address his readers as holy on the basis of their experience or their condition—past, present, or future. What is at stake here is the human creature's *eternal* relation to God, *the* relation in which the person *is* eternal and will become what he certainly never was and *becomes* what he eternally is: God's possession, instrument, servant, and child. This relation is real only because it begins where *everything* comes to an end, in *the* life that comes from death. As the Old Testament continues to teach us, life after death would be a heathen illusion without this ultimate foundation. To address a person as holy in Christ Jesus requires a vantage point wide enough to encompass time and eternity, law and grace, heaven and earth—both in their distinctions from each other and in their relations to each other. Today we are probably only beginning to realize how much we *lack* this vantage point. No wonder that what we preach as the word of God rarely approaches the heights of the message of Ephesians, in spirit or in truth.

We turn now to πιστοί, the second word that Paul uses to designate his readers. It is often said that, in contrast with ἅγιοι, πιστοί denotes the subjective state of the readers; and of course to a certain extent that is correct. Nevertheless, we should treat the concepts "subjective" and "objective" with care when using them to describe the relation between God and human creatures, particularly when interpreting Paul. In this context, what could be subjective that is not also objective? In its most complete sense, ἅγιοι denotes the subjective state of man in the sense that Kierkegaard means when he says that the subjective is the objective.[36] Conversely, the meaning of πιστοί is so closely associated with the object of πίστις that in Romans 3:3 and in many other places in Romans and Galatians it inevitably coincides with this object—without, of course, ceasing to be a human disposition as well. The idea of polarity, equipoise, or balance between divine and human action is absent from Paul's thought; wherever "faith" is spoken of in such a fashion, it leads to simplistic and false dogmatics.

We can avoid this error if we interpret πιστοί in close connection with the more important term ἅγιοι: it refers to those who recognize the divine demands with confident hope. As such, it refers to a truly subjective human state. But keep in mind what is being described here! Where and when do we actually find such recognition, so full of hope? Where, when, and how could faith be a psychological or historical event? Who at any moment could say about oneself, "I believe!" without adding in the same breath, "Dear Lord, help my unbelief?" [cf. Mark 9:24].* Who could answer the question that is put to a person who has been chosen to be God's holy one? Truly, faith is just as much a paradox as holiness is. Faith is the action of the new person in me, the person *I am not*, the new person whose identity within me is the source of the greatest possible honor. Faith is a fundamental and eternal event that is beyond all temporal processes. Faith is God's work in us. It takes place in us, to be sure; it is not some invisible metaphysical reality, independent of our recognition

*The German critical edition includes bracketed scriptural cross-references that were added by the editors. These have been retained in the present edition.

of God's mercy, enclosed in his holiness. But it takes place only as God's work, as the eternal moment hidden within the temporal moment; it is one with what occurs in us. Faith is as pure and original a creation as God's first creation, *creatio ex nihilo*, or it does not deserve to be called πίστις or to be spoken in the same breath as the holiness that Calvin refers to when he says, "*De re infinita nihil potest dici imodice.*"[37] Faith denotes human action, but we must avoid thinking of it as a finite resource, like an expense account that must be replenished when we have spent it.[38] The faith we have to spend is nothing less than this "*res infinita.*" According to the text, a person is ἐν Χριστῷ Ἰησοῦ. With this statement, the text erects the narrow gate of critical negation, through which no one may pass. The *Forward!* command here is preceded by the command *Halt!* The life that opens up before us is preceded by death. This faithfulness comes at precisely the moment when a person is in self-despair—and this includes the religious person. Then, of course, the promise is certain. God remains loyal to his holy ones. This promise is heard only when people recognize God in Christ Jesus as the Lord of life and death, the Lord of lords, the sure foundation and the unfailing hope of those who put their trust in him [cf. Rom. 14:9]. But only in Christ Jesus. In him, the incomparable is spoken.

From this close reading of the text, we are now in the position to understand why Paul dares to refer to his readers as ἁγίοις and πιστοῖς. No historical or pragmatic reasons can adequately account for this risk. It is either foolishness or the ultimate insight into that which gives coherence to human life.

With the phrase τοῖς οὖσιν ἐν Ἐφέσῳ, which stands between ἁγίοις and καὶ πιστοῖς, we venture from *terra firma* to far more uncertain ground.*

1. We begin with the last two words, ἐν Ἐφέσῳ. There is compelling internal and external evidence that they were not part of the original letter. The codices ℵ and B[40] as well as those of Origen, Basil, and Chrysostom provide evidence of an early text without

*At this point, the typescript is set out in the form of notes rather than in complete sentences, as the translation and layout reflect.

this phrase, and the fact that Marcion understood the letter to be addressed to the congregation in Laodicea supports the older text. The internal evidence for the shorter text is that the letter appears to have been addressed to a general audience, without personal knowledge of the recipients;* this is difficult to explain, since Paul was familiar with the community at Ephesus.

2. There is the possibility that the text does not refer to a specific location.

   *Jerome*:[39] τοῖς οὖσιν, those who exist in the metaphysical sense.

   *Bernhard Weiß, Hermann von Soden*: the saints, who are also faithful, in contrast to the covenant community of the Old Testament.

   *J. T. Beck*: those in various congregations who remained loyal in a dispute between Jewish Christians and those following Paul.

   All of that is dubious, given the parallel passages in 2 Corinthians 1:1; Romans 1:7; and Philippians 1:1.

3. Was Marcion correct? Harnack: Yes! Laodicea was deleted, as evidenced by Revelation 3:15ff. But Laodicea was one of the congregations with which Paul was acquainted.
4. A gap needed to be filled. A modern assumption. And why wasn't it preserved in a copy?
5. A circular letter written to various congregations in Asia Minor (on the basis of the reference to Tychicus in 6:21), which, according to Marcion, citing Col. 4:16, included, with Laodicea, the church with the respectable name of Ephesus. By this account, the designation of the congregation was accidentally lost. Unsatisfactory but not at all unlikely.[40]

*Nov. 24, 1921*

At the end of the previous lecture we considered the various possible ways of interpreting the phrase τοῖς οὖσιν ἐν Ἐφέσῳ.† With the newer

*A pencil notation on the margin reads: "6:23–24!"

†In the typescript of the German text, the following is crossed out in pencil: "χάρις is the unheard of conduct of God. God is with us despite us. And εἰρήνη, to be reconciled by the unfathomable will of God, is just as much of a paradox! It is

interpreters, such as Meyer[41] and Haupt, one can accept the phrase ἐν Ἐφέσῳ as authentic, despite the counterevidence of certain early documents and intertextual difficulties. And given the inadequacy of alternate proposals, I confess a certain yearning for this solution. With the ancient church theologians cited by Jerome as well as Hofmann, Beck, Weiß, von Soden, and F. Barth, one can maintain that ἐν Ἐφέσῳ is simply an insertion and try to find another way to deal with the resulting awkward phrase τοῖς οὖσιν καὶ πιστοῖς. One can maintain, with Marcion and Harnack, that the original text read ἐν Λαοδικείᾳ. One can conjecture, as do Bengel[42] and Olshausen,[43] that in the original manuscript the space now occupied by ἐν Ἐφέσῳ was left empty because it was a circular letter. One can maintain, as Jülicher does, that we are dealing with an old manuscript copy, which had been originally addressed to a circle of gentile Christian congregations and accidentally lost. With Dibelius, one can regard the entire epistle as inauthentic and the phrase ἐν Ἐφέσῳ as the work of a redactor, citing 2 Timothy 4:12 as evidence.[44] Finally, as in our recent discussion [*Besprechungsstunde!*],* one can maintain, with Kühl, that a fragment in verse 1 was lost and that τοῖς οὖσιν is a corruption of κλητοῖς οὖσιν (as in Rom. 8:28), in which case ἐν Ἐφέσῳ could be deleted without further difficulties. I believe that I have discharged my duty by making you aware of all these possibilities, and I leave it to you to decide which of them is the least improbable. Because of the inherent problems, the older theologians at any rate avoided extravagant claims about either their methods or their conclusions.

Our greatest difficulty in understanding the familiar apostolic greeting χάρις ὑμῖν in verse 2 is that we know it far too well, or we think that we do. Perhaps if it were censored in all churches for fifty years, we could once again hear it as it was originally intended. The same thing could be said about many other "familiar" Bible words. It is not insignificant that Paul originally coined this formula and used it nearly word for word in all of his letters. Neither the familiar χαίρειν from Greek epistolary salutations nor the formula "grace and

---

not a matter of divine capacity in the first case and human feelings in the second, but truth through God's act, established by God *and* Christ."

*The reference is to one of the weekly seminars that Barth offered in connection with the lectures.

εἰρήνη," the latter of which was roughly equivalent to the Hebrew שלם, were mere conceptual materials for Paul. By changing χαίρειν to χάρις and, more importantly, by linking both terms to the phrase ἀπὸ θεοῦ πατρός . . . , Paul created a characteristically new phrase. His intention was not to form impressive liturgical cadences but to say something of supreme importance, which in fact summarizes his entire message. Χάρις and εἰρήνη both describe conduct that is completely unexpected—God's conduct as well as the creature's. The realities to which these terms refer cannot be taken for granted or assumed. Rather, Paul repeatedly longs for Christians to have a share in these realities. Χάρις is not a state of being; it *comes* and must come ever again. Εἰρήνη is not something we possess like a commodity; we *receive* it and must receive it ever again.

Already in the greeting we are at the heart of Paul's message. His greeting to his congregation, his proclamation to them, is a *reminder*, a prayer for them. It is a reminder of precisely what the finite creature always fails to see, what is always lost on him, what he perennially forgets, but what is always supremely near, always present, always offered so freely and reliably that one need only remember it. In this *prayer* Paul brings to bear his entire personality in order to confront his listeners with this reminder, to say to them what they actually know already, because in the last resort, it is only by personally appealing to God on their behalf that he can tell them the simplest thing of all, which is also the hardest thing of all. (Remember how all the other Pauline letters begin with εὐχαριστῶ τῷ θεῷ or a similar phrase;[45] take a look at εὐλογητὸς ὁ θεός in verses 3–14, the first section of our letter, and you will discover that for Paul the requisite word of *remembrance* directed to the human creature and the word of *prayer* directed to God are inextricably related and fundamentally one.) Right in his greeting Paul says *everything*. As he greets his readers, he points to what is beyond both him and them, what they both lack, and what they can only pray for (and may pray for). Even so, his greeting is a true greeting, an indication of the *community* that exists between them. Because human community exists only on the basis of what is beyond our grasp, a reality for which we can only pray. Nothing self-evident or contingent is an adequate basis for community—only the hidden God and the noncontingent are adequate.

Χάρις refers to God's singular and completely unexpected conduct toward the human creature. God, whom the human creature cannot know at all—because anything that the creature can know is not God; God, who dwells in unapproachable light [cf. 1 Tim. 6:16]; the God, from whom Isaiah recoiled (and with good reason), saying, "Woe is me! For I am lost" [Isa. 6:5]—this *Deus absconditus* is the *Deus revelatus*.[46] Despite ourselves and the fact that we can speak about God only in the form of negation, God nevertheless says *Yes* to this familiar creature, in all his sinfulness, creatureliness, mortality, and absolute godforsakenness. The Absolute is present to this human creature, who possesses no potential, no disposition, and no capacity for the Absolute. (What after all is our "religious instinct" except a question mark that hangs over human existence without providing an answer? Indeed, how can it be anything other than the realization that we are not able to take the first step toward God, not even the smallest baby step? What do we discover from the heights of religion except that the human creature is human?)

On the contrary, what *no eye* has seen, what *no ear* has heard, what *no heart* has imagined—*that* is what God has prepared for those who love him (1 Cor. 2:9). Let us be clear about this: they *become* the ones who love him because he has *prepared* them! It is essential to keep in mind what Rom. 5:5, 8:28, and 1 Corinthians 8:3 say about the source and origin of our love for God. Grace is the grounding of the creature in God. But this grounding is ungrounded; otherwise it would not be grounding in God.[47] Grace is the reality of forgiveness, which has no continuity whatsoever with anything that we can grasp (apart from the continuity that is established by God's will and God's alone!): this human creature, who is fallen and without exception fails to recognize God, is recognized by God as his child. If we really want to think about what the term χάρις refers to, it means that *we cannot do enough*: we cannot elevate God enough in our thoughts, be sufficiently amazed at the unfathomable mystery of his will, or give him enough honor [cf. Deut. 32:3].[48] But then, the divine *Nevertheless*! Despite our *most reverent* thoughts, our *deepest* fear, our *most genuine* amazement, which never even come close to being adequate, despite all this, the surprise, the completely unexpected, unforeseen, incalculable, surprise—incomprehensible (even through the logic of conversion) and unprecedented—as surprising as seeing with our own eyes someone raised from the dead, the wonder of the *reality* of God, in contrast to everything that we think about God: *that* is grace. Paul sees his readers in the light of this great *possibility*. *Grace* is with them. They really are the ἅγιοι καὶ πιστοί.

Can we say more? Can we say that they are *given* grace, that they *have* grace, and that they *stand* in grace? Actually, we *can* say all that, provided we are clear that we can only remember *the reality* of grace and pray for it. "Grace be with you!" I think that Luther hit on something quite original here in his use of the preposition "with."[49] Grace is not poured into a person so that it becomes a possession or an attribute. Grace can only be *with* and accompany a person. The person continues to be what he is, a human being with all that is questionable about him. How could he recognize grace as grace without continually recognizing his own godforsakenness?[50] What makes grace graceful[51] is that God in his majesty is *with* the human being in his creatureliness. If we try to say more than that, we end up saying less.

Likewise, εἰρήνη refers to the human creature's equally singular and unexpected conduct with God. Χάρις and εἰρήνη, which Paul repeatedly and emphatically links, correspond to each other; Paul sees them as the two endpoints of the relation between God and the human creature and the human creature and God, a relation that is infinitely real and therefore never contingent. Εἰρήνη is also a divine *Nevertheless!*, the removal of a barricade, a breakthrough, a victory. Although the conditions for peace do not exist, a peace *settlement* is established (cf. Rom. 5:1ff.). *Even though* the creature remains human, *even though* the sin that separates him from God is infinite and absolute, *even though* there is no creaturely mediation, bridge, or way to God, *even though* from the summit of his existence—I am thinking again about religion—the only thing he learns about himself is that he is a rebel against God, *nevertheless* the human creature is reconciled with God. The unrighteous person we know so well is reconciled with the holy God, whom we do not know! God stands before the creature and the creature before God. God has established a relation with the human creature. Here, the incomprehensible has occurred:[52] time and eternity meet. The human creature is willing, ready, and able to have a renewed [?],* restored, and peaceful relation with God. There comes a point when God, whose hand is raised against the human creature with the power to crush him, relents because he brings the creature's revolt against God (the only thing we can know about our relation to God) to a forceful end. The impossible becomes possible. There is an objective[53] relation between God and the human creature because the infinite distance between the creator and the creature is acknowledged; and precisely because it is acknowledged, it becomes ultimate proximity.[54] That is εἰρήνη, peace.

In the commentaries, peace is often interpreted as a feeling that accompanies a relation with God. One can say that. However, while I have no interest in entering into a dilettante debate about psychology, any more than I do about history, one must avoid saying too little. Anyone who says that peace with God is a feeling must add: a feeling that we cannot recognize and that we *never* experience as such, a feeling that absolutely *transcends* all other feelings. In any case, I must warn you about equating this feeling with what Schleiermacher called "the feeling of absolute dependence,"[55] by which he meant the final and highest human possibility. What feeling, known or imagined, is adequate to grasp this matter? It will necessarily be grounded in what Paul refers to in Philippians 4:7 as the εἰρήνη τοῦ θεοῦ—another all-too-familiar biblical phrase—which he prays will guard, preserve, and keep the hearts of his readers as a soldier guards prisoners, the peace that ὑπερέχουσα πάντα νοῦν. The νοῦς, above which this εἰρήνη towers—and we must add, towers absolutely—includes even the most soaring feelings imaginable. Indeed, the essential elements of εἰρήνη are the thought of *God* and the thought of *eternity*.[56] We can only know what "peace" is on the basis of "*grace*." As Calvin said, God's *acts of creation and redemption* are "the opposite of any capricious, carnal certainty,"[57] the opposite of any pretentious or romantic illusions we may have about grasping the divine fullness, which would amount to seizing what does not belong to us. We have peace with God in the knowledge that *God* is *God* and remains *God*,

*The German critical edition uses bracketed question marks to single out words in Barth's manuscript that are difficult to decipher. These have been retained in the present edition.

in the knowledge that we can *only* believe in God.[58] We can *only* wait and hope without seeing, and this will always be the case. But because the object of our waiting and hoping is God, waiting and hoping constitute our peace with him. Peace with God cannot be attributed to a particular kind of temperament, human attitude, or school of thought. Peace with God can inspire the luminous simplicity of Blumhardt's sermons and prayers[59] just as it can the severity of Kant's *Critique of Pure Reason*; it is neither simplicity nor severity but the meaning that *God* can give to what is profoundly childlike or extraordinarily sophisticated, and which those who are either childlike or sophisticated *lack* until God creates this meaning; consequently, they must continually *receive* it. Notice that *God* is the one who sets out the terms of the peace settlement that this victory has achieved and that it is a true and lasting peace only because God establishes his rule according to his good pleasure. Again, if we tried to say more, we would end up saying less.

Ἀπὸ θεοῦ πατρὸς ἡμῶν καὶ κυρίου Ἰησοῦ Χριστοῦ come both χάρις and εἰρήνη, Paul adds, emphatically. And a few minutes ago, if you were silently wondering how I could say all that I said about χάρις and εἰρήνη, I will tell you: on precisely the same basis as Paul, when he prays for his readers—on the basis of what he expressly brings to their attention. It is *God* we are dealing with here, if these words address us as the author intended. The realities about which they speak are hidden in *God*, and *God* himself guarantees that they are genuine realities. First, we know that we grasp the meaning of the Pauline concepts, and second, we are assured of the reality behind them by following the course indicated by Paul, namely, by listening to and interpreting what is said about God. If we know what we are doing and take the risk of giving to God what is God's, as consistently as possible [cf. Matt. 22:21 par.],[60] we cannot entirely go astray, even though we will, of course, err in certain details.

The most important thing to note for now about the phrase ἀπὸ θεοῦ πατρός . . . I have already pointed out in my explication of χάρις and εἰρήνη. Precisely because Paul attributes the coming of grace and the receiving of peace to God's initiative, he relates the words χάρις and εἰρήνη to God exclusively and radically—or, in terms of our own horizon of experience, unnatural and otherworldly. This is why we must draw attention to the incomprehensible *Nevertheless!* at the heart of both terms. Despite God's holiness, *Grace!* Despite human sin, *Peace!* This is why Calvin's observation "*de re infinita nihil potest dici immodice*" applies to both.[61] I would like to emphasize just two other matters.

*1.* The phrase ἀπὸ θεοῦ πατρὸς ἡμῶν demonstrates in the clearest possible terms that when Paul refers to God as the giver of grace and the source of our peace, he is not thinking about a conspicuous metaphysical object. When he calls God our "Father," he is using the ultimate parable to express the inexpressible and unimaginable, namely, our origin. *Our* origin:[62] *we* human creatures, although thoroughly human, are related to him, who is most wonderful, who is not and never will be simply a contingent object, who is unknown, who is holy, the *Deus absconditus*. When we speak about this God, we are speaking about *ourselves*, about our fundamental *existence*, about the invisible mystery of our visible life, about the θεωρία of our existence, which can never be accounted for by mere πρᾶξις, about the answer that comes from our deepest question. God, who meets us in such an unnatural and unworldly fashion, whose χάρις and εἰρήνη, which must feel to many of you more like a clenched fist than God's generosity and goodness, permeate our daily lives and our individuality—this God is our Father. We all come from him, who is the most distinctive, personal, and universal presupposition of each of us. He, the most wonderful and inaccessible One, appears before our eyes the moment we think of him. It is only as a stranger that we actually know him; it is only when we fear him above all things that we actually love him. Paul's hope is that all these things may actually take place in the lives of his readers: χάρις and εἰρήνη.

2. The phrase καὶ κυρίου demonstrates that the event between God and the human creature, designated by the terms χάρις and εἰρήνη, is not a logical a priori that can be accounted for rationally through terms used in logic, such as "The Not-Given," "ἀνυπόθεσις," "the origin," or any other term one could choose. Instead, it must be described as an event. God is God. God is free. God acts. God reveals himself. There is *knowledge* of God only in light of the *revelation* of God. This action and self-revelation of God are indicated by the strange καί standing between the words "God" and "Jesus." Paul

calls God our Father and the Father of our Lord Jesus Christ, lest Jesus appear to be a second God or half-God alongside the Father. Paul is speaking about the same God in both cases, referring first to his work as God and then to the significance of his work. Because the significance of God's work, namely, the mystery of the creation and redemption of humanity, is the mystery that Paul simultaneously veils and discloses in the expression κύριος Ἰησοῦς Χριστός, here we stand before the final riddle and the final solution that arises from the historical appearance of Christianity and from the problematic of our own life.*

*The following notes are crossed through in pencil: "Abmachung mit Lempp. 25% Christ in der Gesellschaft, Biblische Fragen. Zur inneren Lage. Dostojewski. (Römbr.) stud. Hagemann Testatbuch." Albert Lempp (1884–1943) was the owner of Christian Kaiser Verlag in Munich and Barth's publisher for the Romans commentaries. The marginal note refers to interest in Barth's and Thurneysen's published material, which was still selling briskly at the time. In a letter to Thurneysen on November 27, three days after the lecture was delivered, Barth jests that copies were selling so fast that the publisher could not keep them in stock. See *Karl Barth – Eduard Thurneysen: Briefwechsel II. 1921–1930*, hg. Eduard Thurneysen (Zürich: TVZ, 1987), 14. Barth here refers to his lectures "Der Christ in der Gesellschaft" (1919) and "Biblische Fragen, Einsichten und Ausblicke" (1920). For the English translation of these lectures, see "The Christian's Place in Society" and "Biblical Questions, Insights and Vistas," in *The Word of God and the Word of Man*, trans. Douglas Horton (London: Hodder & Stoughton, 1928), 272–327 and 51–96, respectively.

# EPHESIANS 1:3–14

*Dec. 1, 1921*

[[3] Εὐλογητὸς ὁ θεὸς καὶ πατὴρ τοῦ κυρίου ἡμῶν Ἰησοῦ Χριστοῦ,
ὁ εὐλογήσας ἡμᾶς ἐν πάσῃ εὐλογίᾳ πνευματικῇ ἐν τοῖς ἐπου-
ρανίοις ἐν Χριστῷ, [4] καθὼς ἐξελέξατο ἡμᾶς ἐν αὐτῷ πρὸ κατα-
βολῆς κόσμου, εἶναι ἡμᾶς ἁγίους καὶ ἀμώμους κατενώπιον αὐτοῦ,
ἐν ἀγάπῃ [5] προορίσας ἡμᾶς εἰς υἱοθεσίαν διὰ Ἰησοῦ Χριστοῦ εἰς
αὐτόν, κατὰ τὴν εὐδοκίαν τοῦ θελήματος αὐτοῦ, [6] εἰς ἔπαινον
δόξης τῆς χάριτος αὐτοῦ ἧς ἐχαρίτωσεν ἡμᾶς ἐν τῷ ἠγαπημένῳ,
[7] ἐν ᾧ ἔχομεν τὴν ἀπολύτρωσιν διὰ τοῦ αἵματος αὐτοῦ, τὴν ἄφε-
σιν τῶν παραπτωμάτων, κατὰ τὸ πλοῦτος τῆς χάριτος αὐτοῦ, [8] ἧς
ἐπερίσσευσεν εἰς ἡμᾶς ἐν πάσῃ σοφίᾳ καὶ φρονήσει [9] γνωρίσας
ἡμῖν τὸ μυστήριον τοῦ θελήματος αὐτοῦ, κατὰ τὴν εὐδοκίαν
αὐτοῦ, ἣν προέθετο ἐν αὐτῷ [10] εἰς οἰκονομίαν τοῦ πληρώματος
τῶν καιρῶν· ἀνακεφαλαιώσασθαι τὰ πάντα ἐν τῷ Χριστῷ, τὰ ἐπὶ
τοῖς οὐρανοῖς καὶ τὰ ἐπὶ τῆς γῆς· ἐν αὐτῷ, [11] ἐν ᾧ καὶ ἐκληρώθημεν
προορισθέντες κατὰ πρόθεσιν τοῦ τὰ πάντα ἐνεργοῦντος κατὰ
τὴν βουλὴν τοῦ θελήματος αὐτοῦ, [12] εἰς τὸ εἶναι ἡμᾶς εἰς ἔπαινον
δόξης αὐτοῦ τοὺς προηλπικότας ἐν τῷ Χριστῷ· [13] ἐν ᾧ καὶ ὑμεῖς,
ἀκούσαντες τὸν λόγον τῆς ἀληθείας, τὸ εὐαγγέλιον τῆς σωτηρίας
ὑμῶν, ἐν ᾧ καὶ πιστεύσαντες ἐσφραγίσθητε τῷ πνεύματι τῆς ἐπαγ-
γελίας τῷ ἁγίῳ, [14] ὅς ἐστιν ἀρραβὼν τῆς κληρονομίας ἡμῶν εἰς
ἀπολύτρωσιν τῆς περιποιήσεως, εἰς ἔπαινον τῆς δόξης αὐτοῦ.]

*[3] Blessed be God, the Father of our Lord Jesus Christ, who has blessed us with every spiritual blessing, in heaven, in Christ:*

> 4 *In him, he chose us before the creation of the world to be spotless and blameless before him.* 5 *In love he determined us through Jesus Christ his Son, according to his good pleasure, to exist* 6 *for the praise of the glory of his grace, which he lavished upon us in the beloved.*
>
> 7 *In him we have redemption through his blood, the forgiveness of sins according to the riches of his grace,* 8 *which he has generously given us in perfect wisdom and insight:* 9 *to make known to us the mystery of his will, according to his good pleasure* 10 *(to accomplish in the fullness of time according to his intention) to gather together everything in Christ, the heavenly and the earthly in him.*
>
> 11 *In him we have also become heirs, having been determined (according to the intention of him who accomplishes everything according to the purpose of his will)* 12 *to the praise of his glory to be the first to hope in Christ.*
>
> 13 *In him, you also, having heard the word of truth, the message of your salvation and believing in him, were sealed with the Holy Spirit of promise,* 14 *the downpayment of our inheritance, until it becomes our own possession, to the praise of his glory.*

We begin with an overview of the passage. It is a *doxology*, in which the apostle invites his hearers to praise God along with him, since the praise of God is his subject, and they must adopt the posture of praise in order to grasp it. There is an untranslatable wordplay in verse 3 that trades on the word "blessed," which describes the human act of praise that is required for the readers to understand the writer of the letter: "Blessed be him who has blessed us." This act of praise is described as an echo of what God has done first—both chronologically and in order of importance in the eternal scheme of things—a human echo that follows necessarily and immediately upon the divine action.

Accordingly, all of the ideas in verses 4–14 move between the two poles of the divine action, described as ἐυδοκία, the *beneplacitum* of God, on the one hand, and ἔπαινος, the *glorificatio* of God by the human creature, on the other. The central term εὐλογεῖν, *benedictio*, which occurs throughout verse 3, has a twofold meaning: as the creature recognizes God to be the one who blesses him, he responds by blessing, praising, and glorifying God. As Bengel correctly points out, "Aliter deus benedicit nobis, aliter nos benedicimus illi."[63] An infinite qualitative distinction separates the action of the creator from that of the creature. However, this infinite distinction is precisely what unites the creature and the creator. God can bless man only as his creature; man can bless God only as his creator. The recognition of this infinite distinction is precisely what makes the blessing and the praise both meet and right. Recognition of God's divinity establishes the divine Otherness, the "*aliter*"; and precisely by being established, it is sublated.[64]

It is no accident that Calvin, who understood this relation between God's blessing and human praise better than anyone before or since, seems to have particularly loved verse 3, which sets the tone for the entire epistle.[65] We are created *by* God, from whom we come, and *for* God, toward whom we are moving. We *are standing* on the ground of the *beneplacitum Dei*; we *are moving* toward the goal of the *gloria Dei*. The knowledge of God is the *presupposition*, and the knowledge of God is the *goal* of all human being, having, and doing, including our present speaking and hearing of divine things! This is what Paul wishes to shout to his readers in this doxology. By pointing to both the presupposition and the goal, he means to jolt them out of their constant forgetfulness, to save them from the quicksand of trivialities, to deliver them from both false subjectivity and equally false objectivity by confronting them with the fundamental questions of human existence and the answer that is already given by God. Paul will not allow them to remain as mere spectators and contemplatives; rather, he summons them into the sphere of the subject—to a vocation, a movement, an upheaval, a sublation of time and everything temporal by eternity, in which we come to our senses and walk before God. And all of this takes place in Christ.

The phrase "in Christ" is the actual key to our passage: it appears at the end of verse 3, again in the phrase ἐν αὐτῷ in verse 4, and in the threefold ἐν ᾧ in verses 7, 11, and 13. We should not only recognize this key but also use it vigorously to unlock the meaning of the passage. Accordingly, we use this central motif to arrange the passage in the sequence suggested by Dibelius:[66] *verses 4–6*, Jesus Christ: our election; *verses 7–10*, Jesus Christ: our liberation; *verses 11–12*, Jesus Christ: our hope; *verses 13–14*, Jesus Christ: our sealing with the Spirit. Furthermore, the passage becomes more intelligible if we translate each phrase or sentence that begins with ἐν ᾧ as a separate unit ("In him, he has chosen us [v. 4] . . . In him, we have liberation [v. 7] . . . In him, we are heirs [v. 11] . . . In him you also . . . have been sealed [v. 13]"). This is the only possible way to understand the passage in German. Luther's translation, which preserves all the relative clauses, makes it impossible to grasp the passage as a whole, whether reading it or hearing it read. I strongly recommend accommodating your listeners by using Dibelius's outline in your sermons and Bible studies.

We must remember, of course, that this separation of syntactical units for linguistic clarity runs the risk of obscuring a distinctive feature of the text: the huge span of ideas, expressed in what is for us such a torturing concatenation of clauses, pointing in so many different directions. The early church could express such a span of ideas in a single sentence or thesis as a whole—as a single, rounded truth—because it was regarded as completely integrated and elastic.[67] We must understand the text the same way, not as a collection of dogmatic *loci* but as a single *kerygma*, hearing all the parts simultaneously and each individual part in relation to the others; otherwise, the separation of syntactical units will result in a toning down and a distortion of the contents. In any case, whether we read the original Greek text, Luther's translation, or Dibelius's, let us be sure that we are repeatedly reoriented to the subject by the constantly appearing ἐν ᾧ and the equivalent ἐν Χριστῷ. What is expressed here is not a general, universal truth and therefore cannot be expressed directly—either rationally or irrationally, speculatively or experientially through the vagaries of the "pious consciousness." Rather, it is expressed existentially, indirectly from God and by God, not as individual words in themselves but with every single word in relation to *the* Word, which is not exhausted by any individual word.

Because *that* is the meaning of the phrase ἐν Χριστῷ, it constitutes the formal key to the section. We are placed before *God*, claimed by *God*, born from *God*, and determined for *God*. God himself has blessed us, and for this reason we should praise him. Ἐν Χριστῷ the veil that hides the human creature's true situation, preventing him from seeing that he belongs to God, is torn. Ἐν

Χριστῷ means Immanuel! God with us! [Matt. 1:23]. Ἐν Χριστῷ God draws near in his self-revelation, while remaining distant, strange, and incomprehensible: the *Deus absconditus*. In Christ is thus *the* proximity of God, which always means eternity and never merely the temporal extension of what is palpable, comprehensible, or perceptible. Precisely because the proximity of God is ultimate reality, it can only be believed—and the belief itself is the wonder of its revelation. In Christ are thus election, liberation, hope, and the sealing of the Spirit, says Paul. And he does not mean a series of discrete truths—even holy truths—from which one chooses to affirm some, doubt others, and ignore still others, but rather *the* truth, *the* holiness, which can only be understood temporally in all its variability, in the various concepts of human language, and certainly in the various elements of knowledge and experience. But it can be truly grasped and apprehended as *one*, despite its apparent diversity, but as such as truly *one*, in its totality, in the necessity and solidarity of all its various relations. We are ἐν Χριστῷ; therefore, God has blessed us so that we should praise him. Therein he is the creator and we the creature.

Note well that ἐν Χριστῷ is the *presupposition* and *goal* of our human being, having, and doing—the *beneplacitum Dei* on the one hand and the *glorificatio Dei* on the other—in their original relation, not the human creature's existence or anything he might produce or achieve. Paul would never have described his conversion at Damascus as the cause of his being ἐν Χριστῷ. He was not ἐν Χριστῷ because he experienced Damascus; rather, he experienced Damascus because he was ἐν Χριστῷ. If in an attempt to understand Paul, we reverse the order to conform to our own notions of cause and effect, we will sever the nerve of the passage and forfeit the *only* possible way of understanding the words that sound from the initial κατὰ τὴν εὐδοκίαν τοῦ θελήματος αὐτοῦ and soar to the climactic εἰς ἔπαινον τῆς δόξης αὐτοῦ. As those who we never were, are, or shall be, we are ἐν Χριστῷ; and it is precisely this unprecedented reality—that in Christ we are a new creation—that is incomparable and incommensurable with everything that constitutes our temporal existence. It is this reality that compels his praise to God and about which he intends to remind his readers, as the ἅγιοι καὶ πιστοί, as those who are neither ignorant nor indifferent. Let us turn to the *detailed exposition.**

Concerning εὐλογητός,† it should be noted that for Paul and for the Bible, Old Testament and New, the praise of God is not peripheral, superficial, merely external, or mere lip service. It certainly can become superficial and *will* do so when the object of our praise is no longer God but our own best thoughts, ideas, and wishes; the zenith of human accomplishments; or anything else in the universe, from the least to the greatest. Such putative praise of God is really fundamentally about *us*. It is merely one ordinary activity among others, and easily can be replaced by other concerns. The praise of God to which Paul refers is not a matter of course; it tolerates no rivals. Such praise is directed to God, the Father of Jesus Christ, who reveals himself in his hiddenness and is the creator of all things. It is an act of knowledge, of repentance, of transformed thinking. Something new is opened up in the human creature when he is able to εὐλογεῖν. He has found light where human eyes can only detect darkness. He has made the most important discovery of all. He has found *God*, and he has *found* God. He not only *can* but *must* εὐλογεῖν. "For I can do no other. Woe to me if I do not preach the gospel!" [1 Cor. 9:16].[68] In this context, how could the inward and the outward aspects of praise be separated? How could the praise of God consist of words alone? Words are inadequate, but so is action. We can only cover our faces ("*crever les yeux*," Calvin)[69] and give God the glory.

*Dec. 8, 1921*

Ὁ θεὸς καὶ πατήρ. Καί in this instance (as in Eph. 1:13, καὶ πιστεύσαντες; and Rom. 16:1, καὶ διάκονον) emphasizes πατήρ as that which further clarifies the identity of this θεός. God is praised as *this* God—and as such also as ὁ θεός. *This* God emerges from the ranks of all other gods, real or imagined, as the only one to whom honor is due, as in Athens, the unknown God emerged from the ranks of the known

*Barth comments here: "Gerade bei V. 4 deutlich, daß das Gesagte nicht aus der Luft gegriffen" ("It is clear from v. 4 that what has been said is not out of thin air").

†In the margins, Barth remarks: "Nur Lob? Lob ist gerade genug!" ("Only praise? Praise is just enough!").

gods [Acts 17:23].[70] For Paul, not even monotheism is a self-evident, dogmatic truism; rather, it must be continually rediscovered and re-established. Here, if we are attentive, we discover the vigor behind Paul's ideas: even with the foundations of his "system," he always begins at the beginning and not, like most religious thinkers, with anything assumed or conceded.[71] Nothing is conceded: that God is the *Father of Jesus Christ* and that the Father of Jesus Christ is *God* is as staggering today as it was on day one and must be repeatedly acknowledged and expressed on the basis of continual revelation, not as something known beforehand. What exactly this means for Paul becomes clear in the following clause, which elaborates upon the description of God as Father.

Ὁ εὐλογήσας ἡμᾶς . . . First, we should note the relationship of this εὐλογήσας to the earlier εὐλογητός. As I pointed out earlier, the εὐλογεῖν to which Paul invites his readers is essentially the moment of astonishment. It could just as easily be called joyful discovery as terror. Apart from ἔκστασις, apart from the ecstasy of man face-to-face with the reality of God, there can be no εὐλογεῖν, at least not the kind of praise that is evoked by God. Εὐλογεῖν is the act *of* man, in which God draws near, but as the *unknown* God, whose goodness is *new* every morning [Lam. 3:23]. Εὐλογεῖν is the unmediated act of knowing God that nevertheless emerges originally and wonderfully from not knowing him, an act that in and of itself is nothing other than a qualified, prolonged [?] not knowing of God, a *docta ignoranta*,[72] an awe-inspired adoration of God in his divinity, that is, in his unfathomable majesty. Therefore when God reveals himself in Christ, he reveals himself in absolute mystery, in contrast to all that is known or simply given. He is *revelatus* as *absconditus*.

This interpretation of the εὐλογητός seems unavoidable, given its relationship to the εὐλογήσας that is spoken by God and to everything else that is said in verses 4–14. The creature's eternal election, redemption, appointment to hope, and anointing by the Holy Spirit constitute the *divine* act that Paul refers to as εὐλογεῖν. *Human* εὐλογεῖν means the act by which the creature becomes *objective* before God and stands in the place where God draws near. Think about what this means! Clearly it is a profound ecstasy, more profound than any ecstasy that we can account for psychologically, an act in which a person radically transcends what is humanly possible. Could the creature be objective before God at one moment just as much as the next? Could the creature make the radically new beginning at any given moment? Couldn't the εὐλογεῖν at any moment signify the unprecedented transformation, the act that brings light out of darkness, a sublation of time? No, says Paul: the origin, spontaneity, and essence of the human εὐλογεῖν lie neither in the creature nor in creaturely time. Rather, God appears first with *his* εὐλογεῖν. Human εὐλογεῖν is a response to *his* call. *His* freedom is the sphere in which the creature acquires the freedom for such an act. *This* incomparable human possibility emerges from all possible human achievements just as radically as God himself emerges from the ranks of other gods. This explains the necessity for the human creature's praise of God and the vigor with which the creature is claimed for the glory of God. Praise, the divine possibility for man, which is beyond description and beyond all human boundaries, nevertheless becomes an actual reality for the creature. The divine possibility is a *necessity*. It manifests itself as an *absolute* act, *tout court*.

Note that the *divine* act of blessing in which this human act is grounded is described as *speech*. God blesses. He *speaks* a *word* of promise and a *word* of grace. That is all. No *gratia infusa*.[73] No direct *communication* of life. No direct relationship between God's will and what occurs in the world, within man, or among human affairs. Not a creative *act* but, as in Genesis, the creative *word*. He *speaks*, and it comes to be; he *commands*, and it stands firm [Ps. 33:9]. The word *alone* does it. In the word as *word*, every conceivable act is included. As divine *word*, God's εὐλογεῖν becomes the ground of and occasion for the human creature's εὐλογεῖν. If the divine possibility for man does not appear as *word*—with the utter strangeness and distinctiveness of the word, which cannot be understood directly—it does not appear at all. If is it not believed as *word*, it will not be believed at all. If it is not *the* possibility, which can only be *believed*, it is not the *divine* possibility for man. As *God's* possibility for the creature, it can only be *believed*. The New Testament λόγος is *not* simply the supreme form of humanly mediated reality or any kind of material *hypostasis*; rather, it refers to the relation in which God confronts man directly. Λογίζεσθαι and here εὐλογεῖν [denote][74] *not* to any kind of a priori relation but to the divinely created relation between God and man. Εὐλογεῖν therefore refers to the divine act as an undifferentiated, unexpected, free act of absolute revelation. As such, the divine word calls the human creature out of himself and into the world of the Father of Jesus Christ, into the world of freedom.

The threefold use of the preposition ἐν points us in the same direction. Following Hofmann, I think it simplest and best to form three parallel sentences, each beginning with ἐν rather than forming three subordinate clauses. Unlike the majority of commentators, I see nothing in the text that requires a syntactical relationship between only the first two ἐν-clauses; and it seems to me that the meaning of the passage emerges most clearly if instead we separate each ἐν-clause with a comma and imagine all three as a circle, proceeding from the central εὐλογήσας. Before considering the nature of that blessing, we must describe the manner in which God blesses the creature. God blesses (1) with every blessing of the Spirit, (2) in heaven, (3) in Christ. If this gives the impression of saying the same thing three times, then we are on the right track: the blessing proceeds from the center of the same circle three times, albeit in three distinctive ways.

Ἐν πάσῃ εὐλογίᾳ πνευματικῇ. The play on words with εὐλογεῖν appears once again. "God blesses us with blessings—and for this we are blessed!" Unless we assume that Paul wrote in a deliberately stylized fashion simply to sound poetic, then it should be obvious that the Pauline message is intentionally and thoroughly dialectical and must be understood dialectically. Do not be led astray by the current voices clamoring for simplicity,[75] particularly by those who without any basis contrast the dialectical Paul with the allegedly simple Jesus.[76] The goal of dialectical communication is simplicity, that is, the truth, that is, God. But God must be *believed* as God, and God can *only* be believed. Therefore, all authentic communication about him is necessarily dialectical, that is, broken, indirect, pointing beyond itself.[77] *We* are not so simple that we can receive a simple communication about simplicity. *Our* alleged simplicity is ever-increasing complexity and confusion. We can be open to the divine simplicity only if we are profoundly unsettled in our human simplicity. Therefore, do not think that dialectic is a special feature of Paul that can be dismissed with the catchword "Paulinism." Dialectical theology is behind the best of Luther's early sermons and table talk. Most importantly, Jesus's speech is supremely dialectical. I would go so far as to say that Jesus's speech is even more dialectical than Paul's, precisely because his words, which at first sound so simple and direct, are actually so suggestive and laden with meaning. Whenever we speak about God, what is meant differs from what is said; and the more truly we speak about God, the greater is the difference between what we mean and what we say. And that is precisely why dialectical communication is so infinitely instructive and infinitely vexing for the interpreter. Whoever prefers to avoid it should know that he prefers not to hear about God. Whoever *intends* to hear about God, in whom we can *only* believe—whoever would hear afresh that God is the one in whom one can only *believe*—will certainly not avoid dialectical communication because he understands that it is the only adequate form of communication.

"God blesses us with *blessings*." The blessing of the divine word is itself a word, *only* a word, *only* a promise, *only* a pledge, whose fulfillment we do not see. If we saw the fulfillment, the promise would not be *God's* promise. If in giving his gift, God ceased to be a mystery, then the gift would not be *God's* gift. No, *we* will never plumb the depths of God's blessing. It will always elude our grasp. It is never at our beck and call. The New Testament *plerophory*[78] does not mean that we have advanced beyond Abraham, as if somehow we had more than the *word* or are required to do more than to *believe*. Rather it means that in Christ, the blessing of Abraham is recognized as the blessing under which *all* persons in *all* generations stand [cf. Rom. 4:9–12, 16–18; Gal. 3:6–9, 14]. It means that in Christ, the word of God is recognized as the divine and therefore the universal possibility for all persons in all times and for all peoples. It means that in Christ faith is freed from the common perception that it is merely one among other historical religions instead of the presupposition from which we all come and which we need only realize in order to enter into the generation that is blessed on account of Abraham. But blessing remains blessing. Word remains word. Faith remains faith.[79] Even in light of the New Testament fullness, man remains man, and the world remains the world, just as the advent of the fullness of time in Christ affords no direct insight into its fullness for those who live in time—no direct insight into the coming of the new heaven and the new earth. "My grace *is sufficient* for you"! [cf. 2 Cor. 12:9].[80]

To want more in this case is to want less. It is a *heathen* plerophory that promises more than the blessing of God, that promises the presence of God in the form of visible, direct immediacy, which is the domain of gods and idols. Here, where the point is how God *has* blessed us, let us take care not to hanker after what is not properly ours and thereby forfeit what we do have and are allowed to have.[81] God blesses us with blessings. Any train that attempts to ignore this *Halt!* signal is derailed, as church history testifies a thousand times over. But, it is "with the blessings of the *Spirit*" that God blesses us. And with that, the unheard of is indeed declared: God's unmediated presence for us, for you and for me, God in his inapproachability, inaccessibility, and hiddenness. God, who cannot be known, surrounds, besieges, storms, and reorders the domain of my knowing. At the limits of my intellectual powers, of my strength of character and disposition, stands the power of God, who is both the final question and the final answer. My existence borders God's existence, verging not upon a separate existence but upon the inverse of my own nonbeing, the ultimate *Aufhebung* and grounding of my own existence.[82] My personality is found as it is lost and lost as it is found in the ultimate reality of God's personality.[83] God speaks. What does my speaking or my silence amount to? God acts. What is the source of my own action or nonaction? God is in the right. What difference does it make if I am in the right or not? God lives. What is the significance of my own life and death? Knowing this does not obliterate, neutralize, or obviate anything that is mine, positive or negative; but the relativity of all that is mine is clearly revealed, or to be precise, *related* to its origin, measured according to the standard by which all things are decided, large and small, life and death, good and evil. What I am, I am in relation to God.

What is intrinsically mine may stand under grace or law, but this is a secondary question that must be decided on a case-by-case basis; and [it must be said][84] that in every case both grace and law are relevant. Let us establish this as fundamental: God gives us the Spirit, we are related to him, without whom we are nothing and with whom we are everything that he is himself. God *gives* us the Spirit. Then how could our relationship with God at any moment be based on anything that is already given, or on the object of either rational knowledge or irrational feeling? No, *this* point in us, the Spirit of God, is not accessible by either rational or irrational paths. The Spirit is not accessible at all; he is the absolute Other. Our greatest spiritual capacity, including the supremely religious achievements of our spirit in the world, stands diametrically opposed to him. He is God's creative act among us, not one act among others—certainly not an act that we can imagine by recourse[85] to anything visible, material, or temporal—but rather God's creative act as God's *word*, God's λόγος, God's own Spirit, meaning, and ground. So, with a *word* of blessing that proceeds from the Spirit, God blesses us. It has been so from the beginning: God's *word* alone stands. Word, not act (despite what Goethe says).[86] The act only in the *word*, the *word* as act, which should be a sufficient guarantee that in his Spirit God blesses us with his supremely real presence.

The boundlessness of this εὐλογία, or state of blessedness, is what Paul emphasizes when he says that God blesses us with *every* blessing of the Spirit. Haupt's translation of εὐλογία πνευματική as "blessing from the religious realm" conveys almost the opposite meaning. When speaking of the Spirit, we can no longer maintain such distinctions between discrete domains; and it is precisely when the Spirit is *absent* that such distinctions are made and the Spirit is confined to the "religious realm." What do concepts like "religious" and "realm" mean when we are speaking about the human relationship to God? Only to the extent that the relationship is *absent* does such a delimitation have meaning; and where the relationship does exist, this delimitation is removed. The Spirit is the attack on all human being, having, and doing, including both the predicament and the promise of all things human. Take away the Spirit—that is, the relationship in which our predicament and promise are grounded in God—and the negative consequences tend to be just as bitter in the scientific, artistic, and political realms as in the "religious realm." In the New Testament, therefore, the correlate of the Spirit is the resurrection of the body (Rom. 8:11), by which the totality of our existence and essence are determined by our relationship with God. Because the divine word of blessing with which we are blessed is a πνευματικὴ εὐλογία, it is necessarily πᾶσα. By contrast, a merely religious εὐλογία is not worthy of the designation πνευματική and is certainly not the word of blessing that encompasses the full extent of human extremity.

Ἐν τοῖς ἐπουρανίοις. The phrase—it means the same as the noun τὰ ἐπουράνια in normal Pauline usage—occurs in the New Testament only in Ephesians (cf. 1:20; 2:6; 3:10; 6:12); and in each case, the meaning is *locative*.[87] Christ is seated at God's right hand in heaven (1:20) and we with him (2:6). Through the existence of the ἐκκλησία, the wisdom of God is revealed to the powers and principalities who are in heaven (3:10), as are the πνευματικὰ τῆς πονηρίας with which we must contend (6:12). In light of these parallels, we must reject the suggestion of Beck and others to translate it "God has blessed us with heavenly *possessions*." Rather, as already shown regarding the paradoxical εὐλογία, Paul again emphasizes that this is *God's* blessing, which can only be given to us. Calvin's interpretation points us in the right direction: "Voluit indicare *praestantiam* gratiae quae per Christum nobis confertur."[88] In the most spacious of all rooms, as Hofmann says rather well,[89] the decisive word is spoken, and the decision turns out to be favorable for us. Every good and perfect gift comes from *above*, as James puts it [James 1:17]. Clearly Paul thinks about this "above" as a battlefield: on one side is Christ the field marshal, standing at the king's right hand [cf. 1:20–22], and we with him; on the other side are the principalities and powers [cf. 6:12], which are alienated from God and opposed to him, in their utter disarray, exercising their limited influence. Here, as in chapter 6, Paul says that the origin of our current predicament is the same as that of the divine blessing, namely, the promise of victory. We should not be put off by the figurative quality of Paul's words, which provides grounds for neither metaphysical speculation nor rationalistic rejection of the ideas behind them. Throughout the passage, Paul is thinking from a human point of view. The riddle confronting us here, like the fact that we can recognize God only in his word, is that we see God and our relationship with him in light of the "not yet," the victory that is not yet complete. But even from this darkness, ἐπουράνια heralds the last word, εὐλογία, the promise—that nothing can separate us from the love of God [cf. Rom. 8:39].

And all this, finally and emphatically: ἐν Χριστῷ.[90]

*Dec. 15, 1921*

Καθώς (v. 4)* functions like a colon that introduces the words that follow. Strictly speaking, it is part of the syntactical unit that comprises verses 4–6, but I would in fact relate it to the entire section (vv. 4–14). God has blessed us in Christ with every blessing of the Spirit in heaven: καθώς, *that is*, he has chosen us in him; we have redemption in him; we are heirs in him; we are those who wait for the salvation that is to come; and all of this you share with us. As I said in the previous lecture, I would outline the entire passage as follows: There is the blessing of God, from which *we come*, namely, ἐκλογή (vv. 4–6). There is the blessing of God in which we *stand*, namely, ἀπολύτρωσις, the forgiveness of sins (vv. 7–10). And there is the blessing of God for which *we are headed*, namely, the future κληρονομία for which we hope, developed in two different formulations (vv. 11–12 and vv. 13–14). Note well that this succession of three or four trains of thought does not constitute three different truths. Nor does their relationship consist in the fact that they constitute a plan, method, or history. Rather, a single truth is expressed here in three distinct forms, and the distinct meaning of each individual form can be understood only by noting how each relates to their common origin. What relates this succession of thought forms is that each in turn depicts what cannot be depicted: the single act of God, his

*The following comments in the margin appear to be Barth's notes for an announcement prior to the lecture: "Complaint: too slow; text: not simple, not insignificant, not first controversy. *Understand*: to understand something from the word, no control how far to understand or not to understand." The following is an attempt to reconstruct Barth's announcement based on the notes: "Announcement: In response to the complaints that we are moving too slowly, I would point out that the text we are considering is not easy to interpret, not insignificant, and not merely a matter of controversy. Our goal is to *understand* the text. We have no control over how far we go or do not go when it is a matter of understanding something from the word." By this point in the course, Barth had delivered five lectures, roughly one half of the semester, and covered only three verses. We have evidence from the announcement prior to the third lecture, on November 24, that he realized that he would not be able to cover the entire epistle. This announcement suggests that he did not know how much of the letter he would cover until the end of the course (see below for his comments about the necessity of summarizing chapters 2–6 in a final lecture). In the Calvin lectures, he faced a similar challenge. At some point in the semester, he realized that he would not be able to cover the material that he had announced and would need to alter his approach. See Barth, *Theology of John Calvin*, xvi–xvii.

εὐλογεῖν ἐν πάσῃ εὐλογίᾳ πνευματικῇ, ἐν τοῖς ἐπουρανίοις, ἐν Χριστῷ. In view of the single act of God, we can (with Calvin) emphasize the blessing of God from which we come, and therefore the God who predestines. We can (with Luther and many others) place the emphasis on the blessing of God in which we stand, on the forgiveness of sins. Or, finally, we can place the emphasis (with Blumhardt, for example) on the blessing of God to which we are headed so that we emphasize eschatology.

The decisive thing with each of these distinctive emphases is that we know what we are doing and why, namely, that with the perceptible, temporal truth with which we speak, we actually mean the one, imperceptible, eternal act of God. Part of the greatness of the theology of the Reformers is that precisely *because* they grasped the truth so one-sidedly, they express this ultimate relationship to the origin so clearly and precisely. Let us not abandon this one-sidedness too quickly. To become as universal as Paul, we must first become one-sided! The possibility of formulating and depicting each of the various forms of the truth with equal seriousness, as equally significant and important—the possibility of being, say, Calvin, Luther, and Blumhardt simultaneously—is either an intellectual feat of the first order or a more or less mindless, unoriginal compendium. Whether the endeavor of dogmatics—which as you know is the attempt to form an ordered relation of the various truth forms—turns out to be an intellectual feat of the first order or a mindless, unoriginal compendium must, of course, be assessed on a case-by-case basis. In any case, we should be aware as dogmaticians—and it is well known that secretly everyone is a dogmatician—that it is no small matter to form an ordered relation of all truths and thereby to speak truly and earnestly. The best way to avoid a mindless compendium is to begin with an intellectual act of the second order, that is, to start with *one* of the possible truth forms, not with the intention of remaining there (neither Calvin nor Luther nor Blumhardt did that, to mention them again) but rather from a single starting point to propose a survey of all the possible viewpoints by showing how each individual viewpoint is related to the origin.

In our section, Paul speaks on the basis of such a panoramic view. He speaks from the limits that we can attain only with great difficulty.

If we want to understand him, we must *anticipate* a vantage point that presumably not a single one of us here has attained. Our actual viewpoint of the divine blessing in Christ will include only a small sector of the circle described here. However, let us read Paul so that through such anticipation we can at least be sure that our small sector is truly part of the *circle*. We should try to understand as *one* reality what Paul presents successively as election, reconciliation, hope. Paul indicates that he understands everything to be truly *one* both formally, by enclosing all three within the phrase ἐν ᾧ or ἐν Χριστῷ, and materially, by what he says about each individual part.

Ἐξελέξατο. Ἐκλέγεσθαι means to pick out, select, or choose. To understand what Paul means here, we should be wary about jumping to the conclusion, as Calvin does, that this election is necessarily a double election, that the election to be ἅγιος and ἄμωμος, which is described here, necessitates a corresponding election to condemnation.[91] We should be just as wary of the more or less forced attempts of many recent exegetes to avoid this obvious implication by contending, as do Hofmann[92] and Ritschl,[93] that the object of election is actually the church of Christ; or, with Beck,[94] all of humanity rather than individuals; or by minimizing the seriousness of this implication by saying, as does Philipp Matthäus Hahn (*Erbauungsstunden über den Brief an die Epheser*, 1878),[95] that election merely indicates the order in which God reveals himself, first to one person, then to another; or, with Haupt, that "the κλῆσις is only the projection of an event occurring in time."[96]

The weakness of all of these interpretations, including Calvin's to a large extent, is that they stem from anthropological concerns. Can there be, may there be, must there be *individuals* chosen for condemnation in addition to those chosen for blessedness? That is the question behind these interpretations. Yes, says Calvin. He once preached on double predestination from this text for literally almost an entire day: a long sermon in the morning followed by an even longer one in the afternoon,[97] claiming that this teaching has "utilité si grande, qu'il vaudroit mieux que nous ne fussions pas nais, que dèstre ignorants de ce que S. Paul nous declare ici," and even further that, "qu'il vaudroit mieux que tout le monde fust abysmé, que de se taire de ceste doctrine."[98] Undoubtedly, Calvin's yes is closer to Paul's meaning than the other exegetes' variously qualified no. When forced to answer the anthropological question, Paul also responded with an unqualified yes, though I do not intend to introduce Romans 9 here.[99] But the actual significance of predestination—and in this regard even Calvin occasionally departs from Paul—is *not* to be found in this anthropological question, not for Paul and finally not even for Calvin. For Paul, the statement *God chooses!* is primarily a statement about God—indeed, about God's relationship with the human creature and, more precisely, about *God's* relationship with the human creature. When in the presence of Christ Paul attempted to answer the question *Who am I? Where do I as one blessed by God come from?*, he answered, *I have been chosen by God!* This statement includes the possibility that I am *not* chosen or that I am chosen for unbelief and condemnation because I might not be recognized in the presence of Jesus Christ. Therefore the possibility and even the reality of double predestination cannot be disputed. To this extent, Calvin is right.

But with Paul a lot depends on the objectivity with which he expresses this ἐκλέγεσθαι of God; because of this objectivity, he is not compelled to point out or describe every situation in which both sides of predestination are either possible or impossible. He is concerned about the double predestination of the human creature in *God*, not about the double predestination of the *human creature*. His outstretched finger points above, not below.[100] By contrast, in the Calvinist doctrine of predestination—at least as Calvin expressed it dogmatically and homiletically—psychological concerns already cast their shadow, and this feature is evident in Calvin's imitators following the Reformation and in subsequent periods. Because the "utilité de cette doctrine,"[101] as Calvin develops in detail, is that this doctrine alone truly humbles the creature and brings assurance of salvation, the interpretation of ἐκλέγεσθαι undergirding the doctrine necessarily reveals the electing God in his unfathomable freedom, sovereignty, and majesty. *He* chooses, he *only*, he himself, and he alone. *He* is recognized as our origin because *he* humbles us, sending us back to the dust,[102] and exalts us in the community of his glory. *This* is how he reveals himself in Christ, as utterly remote, as the King of kings and Lord of lords [cf. Rev. 17:14; 19:16], the origin of our origins. Because *that* is the fundamental meaning of the Calvinist doctrine of predestination and what constantly shines through. Despite the psychological elements, Calvin and his doctrine tower above all those recent theological lightweights who have forgotten the meaning of "*soli Deo gloria.*" And precisely the mature insight that *that* is the basic meaning of his doctrine could have spared Calvin himself many forced and artificial explanations. The claim that the double predestination of the *human creature tout court* effectively humbles and assures him might prove to be forced and artificial; and to the extent that more recent theology is interested fundamentally only in the religious situation of man in and of himself, it is more correct than Calvin. It needs to understand, however, that Calvin's position is wrong precisely at the point that it is eroded by embracing the assumptions of more recent theology. We must first understand Paul, bypassing Calvin, in order to understand Paul by way of Calvin; but we will understand neither by approaching the question in a way that seems commonplace or plausible to us.

Everything else in verses 4–6 is merely a description and explanation of this ἐξελέξατο. It should be obvious that in this section, Paul is describing one segment of a circle.

Ἐν αὐτῷ, in Christ, God has chosen us, Paul says. Who is this αὐτός, this Christ, in the relationship? Clearly, he is God's grasp upon the individual whom God summons: not humanity in general but a *particular* person according to God's *choice*, not this or that person on account of one human quality or another but a particular person according to *God's* choice, not this or that human circle or any group that is distinguished qua group but, once again, *God's* choice upon *these particular* people in all of their individuality and uniqueness.[103] Christ is not a generic term for humanity, church, people group, or corporation but is the Individual, Unique One—in his individuality and uniqueness before *God*, however—the historical one who is eternal, the Son of Man who is the Son of God. In him we recognize God as *our* God, who turns to us in complete freedom because in him God *himself* is given and recognized. Ἐν αὐτῷ does diminish the *wonder* of election; no bridge is built from eternity to time, from God to the human creature. Eternity remains eternity, and God remains God; what occurs and is revealed in Christ is that man, who lives in time, also lives in God, who by nature lives and remains in eternity.

God turns to the human creature as the God who elects in absolute freedom, but in this way he truly turns to the creature. "Si in Christo sumus electi, ergo extra nos" (Calvin), but "*sumus electi.*"[104] Everything depends on continually recognizing the enormous tension that exists in this ἐν αὐτῷ. Are we chosen? Yes, we are chosen by God, whom we do not choose and have never chosen; we are chosen as these particular people in *this* time in *this* world, and only in this way.

Πρὸ καταβολῆς κόσμου. These words safeguard Paul's understanding of election from any possible confusion with fate, nature, or history. No relationship in time, in the world, in history—not even a historical connection with Jesus—assures this relation as securely as does election in Christ, however assured we may be in all of these other relations. We should recognize, however, that there is a relation beyond all relations, an ultimate synthesis. That is what meets us in Jesus Christ. Our ἐκλογή, the *Yes* that God speaks to us, is rooted in this synthesis. He is beyond time, beyond the world, beyond all causality, though not as the *prima causa* of the first of a series. Paul's doctrine of predestination is more sharply formulated than both Augustine's and the Reformers'. It is not a question of being chosen as the member of a group; rather, God chooses as the One and Only. As the eternal One, he chooses the human creature, who lives in time. In this decisive moment of God's *freedom*, emphasized here by ἐκλέγεσθαι, God is distinguished from all random events, gods, and idols. We should not confuse any contingency in the κόσμος with *this* contingency, because this is the contingency that exists through what is noncontingent. Its grounding πρὸ καταβολῆς κόσμου must be sought yesterday, today, tomorrow, and ever again. God is alive, not an impersonal, immovable principle. His election is not a form of natural law but the law of freedom. That is what is conveyed here.

*Jan. 12, 1922*

We resume with the infinitive phrase in verse 4, εἶναι ἡμᾶς ἁγίους καὶ ἀμώμους κατενώπιον αὐτοῦ. The divine ἐκλέγεσθαι is directed toward a particular dimension of human existence: being holy and blameless before him, for this he has chosen us. Our existence before him as the elect, summarized in the expression εἰς υἱοθεσίαν in verse 5, is the proximate temporal purpose willed by God and achieved in Christ, which anticipates the accomplishment of his final, eternal purpose, expressed in the phrase εἰς ἔπαινον δόξης τῆς χάριτος αὐτοῦ (v. 6). It is thus a complete circle that Paul envisions: from the mystery of God's own counsel and will, his purpose proceeds to us known, perceptible, utterly finite human creatures and beyond us, before returning to the mystery itself, that we, his children, are to be holy and blameless before him so that the glory of grace may be praised. The human creature is the arena of action of the Unique One,[105] who is his own purpose and goal. *We* are only the arena; nevertheless, we are the *arena*. That is what is promised to us here.

As I said last time, the interpretation of ἁγίους καὶ ἀμώμους is disputed. J. T. Beck argues, with characteristic liveliness, that the phrase refers to the "ethical character" that is established for "humanity chosen in Christ through the determination to election in Christ before the world was created."[106] I cannot go with Beck here, nor do the majority of commentators, because of the context from verse 3 on, in which εἶναι ἁγίους καὶ ἀμώμους is parallel to εἰς υἱοθεσίαν as well as to the corresponding passage in Colossians (Col. 1:22). This context provides clear evidence for the view that "verse 4 speaks of God's conduct with the human creature, not of the human creature's conduct with God" (Haupt).[107] However, I think that von Soden is cavalier to say, in sharp contrast to Beck, that what is described here is "only the religious relation."[108] Expressions such as εἶναι ἡμᾶς ἁγίους καὶ ἀμώμους are intended to be taken empirically, and in this respect Beck's intention is undoubtedly correct. Presumably Paul would find unintelligible such meticulous distinctions between the religious and the ethical realms. For him, the reality of God is a *single* sphere.

Therefore, it is beyond dispute that God's intention for us, which is described here, is an unprecedented attack on man, upon the entirety of man, an attack whose effects are certainly not limited to what we normally refer to as the ethical realm. Remember what we said about ἅγιος in the first lecture. A person who is chosen by God and therefore God's holy one, a prophet or apostle, for example, is shaken down the line and thrown off track in much more than his religious relation.[109] It is utterly impossible that what the hidden God accomplishes in the person will not also have the greatest visible consequences in that person's life. It is utterly impossible for faith not to be accompanied by good works, as Luther says. The seismic tremor that shakes the human creature's trust in the things of the world and the moral appeal to the human creature to "Become what you are!" at the heart of this infinitive clause are unmistakable; but what is even clearer is the phrase κατενώπιον αὐτοῦ, holy and blameless in God's presence. In his presence, everything human is shaken and wounded, including all good works, even the greatest prophetic or apostolic holiness. They are called into question as human work, which can be quantified and qualified. When we have done everything that is required of us, we can only say that we are useless servants! [Luke 17:10]. Ἅγιοι καὶ ἄμωμοι, or δίκαιοι, the term that Paul uses regularly in his earlier letters [cf. Rom. 2:13; 5:19; also Rom. 1:17; 3:26; Gal. 3:11], refer to the world of sin understood through the reality that God forgives us because of what we have become and is pleased with us as we are, that is, those whose existence is determined by the judgment of God. *That* is the happy Christian proclamation. Who could hear it and walk away undisturbed or remain the same? Conversely, who could hear it and mistake the little disturbance and transformation that it effects in him for the imputed, forensic, alien righteousness that is ascribed to us in Christ? "Gloria Dei summus est finis, cui nostra sanctificatio est subordinata" (Calvin).[110] This "summus finis"[111] is applicable from beginning to end: from *beginning*, by making impossible the assurance that is based on "only [a] religious relation," to *end*, by making equally impossible the existence of an ethical habitus. Man qua man is always impossible. Human possibility is found only in the faith and obedience in which man recognizes himself in light of that which is overcome. What is possible is God alone, who intercedes for man in Christ.[112]

The participial phrase in verse 5, ἐν ἀγάπῃ προορίσας ἡμᾶς εἰς υἱοθεσίαν διὰ Ἰησοῦ Χριστοῦ εἰς αὐτόν, is a second iteration of the same idea. I agree with most recent exegetes that ἐν ἀγάπῃ modifies the phrase that follows it, but with a qualification. I do not think we can rule out the possibility that the phrase refers to the human creature's love for God as the correlate of divine election, as in Romans 8:28. The evidence for this reading is that the parallel phrase in verse 8, ἐν πάσῃ σοφίᾳ καὶ φρονήσει, *cannot* modify the phrase that follows. On this reading of Ephesians, human love for God would be associated with εἶναι ἁγίους καὶ ἀμώμους, in contrast to these objective, "juristic" human characteristics,[113] and would refer to the unprecedented human act by which the divine act is affirmed and grasped, just as love for God is poured into our hearts through the Holy Spirit, according to Romans 5:5, as I understand it.[114] However, the evidence against this interpretation is that such a syntactical relation between ἐν ἀγάπῃ and ἁγίους καὶ ἀμώμους is unattested. Above all, it does not fit the context of the passage as a whole, in which human action plays no sustained role, because the emphasis is on the praise of the divine εὐλογία.

We will therefore interpret ἀγάπη as God's love *for us* and read the phrase as follows: In love, God determined that we should be his children through Jesus Christ. The sovereign freedom and lordly power of God, who conducts himself toward us solely as the electing God, whose act of electing must be understood as an entirely absolute action from beginning to end, is revealed in Jesus Christ as love. The *Deus absconditus* is revealed as our Father. There is no cause to shudder as before a despot, because his despotism is the despotism of love. In love he determines what happens to us according to the good pleasure of his will, as it says later. Προορίζειν is synonymous with ἐκλέγεσθαι, just as the Latin *praedestinatio* is synonymous with *electio*. Both are pictures, indeed anthropomorphic pictures, of the sovereignty by which God has created a relation with us: προορίζειν emphasizes the divine will in itself, ἐκλέγεσθαι his absolute freedom. Προγινώσκειν, which appears in Romans 8:29, emphasizes the knowledge of God that anticipates all actual events[115] and in this way guards the divine sovereignty from being mistaken for necessity, fate, or natural causes.

So it is certain that God has determined in love that we are εἰς υἱοθεσίαν εἰς αὐτόν. In Haupt's commentary, you find the exceedingly awkward translation, "being made into a child."[116] But it actually strikes exactly the right emphasis. We do not become God's children either by process or procreation.[117] When we become children of God, there is a new creation, a new birth. But we must become his children. The good news of our kinship with God is not a direct communication. It is *never* based on experience; its confirmation is *never* based on an unmediated, innately spiritual connection between a person and God. The relation presupposes an infinite abyss between the creator and the created. Ὑιοθεσία is a strange, new event, completely distinct from everything in our familiar way of life. It means that the estranged from God become children of God by adoption.[118] Ὑιοθεσία is creation out of nothing. Becoming God's children occurs by divine appointment, according to divine will, through an event that takes place διὰ Ἰησοῦ Χριστοῦ. There is one begotten Son of God. He stands facing us, the image of our own existence through divinely appointed sonship—not κατὰ σάρκα, not ἐκ σπέρματος Δαυείδ, but κατὰ πνεῦμα ἁγιωσύνης ἐξ ἀναστάσεως νεκρῶν (Rom. 1:3–4), and ἐν δυνάμει, by *God's* appointment[119]—a sonship unlike any human sonship and that only *God* can give and that God *does give* to those whom he wills and determines to become his children. Dibelius says that kinship with Christ is "experienced."[120] We can say that, as long as we add: "experience" that we do not experience except as promise. How could the experience of the Son of God, that is, of the risen one, the experience of the new man who is begotten by God for us, be anything except promise, since all of these experiences surpass even our greatest experience? The promise of our υἱοθεσία includes the promise of the Holy Spirit, the resurrection of the dead, and the fulfillment of everything that God wills and determines concerning us. That, Paul says, is what is given to us in Jesus Christ. Through Jesus Christ we encounter the God who intercedes for us and therefore makes faith and obedience possible.

But, understand clearly, Paul adds immediately, this possibility is God's possibility; and he establishes this claim by describing the promise given to us as *God's* promise. God wills and determines that we should become his children κατὰ τὴν εὐδοκίαν τοῦ θελήματος αὐτοῦ. Εὐδοκία, the good pleasure of his will,[121] is not merely a second, weaker description of ἐν ἀγάπῃ. It means being loved and esteemed freely by God. "Gratuito non mercenario amore Deus nos complectitur" (Calvin); and "Dominus nos adoptando, non respicit quales simus, nec conciliatur nobis ulla personae nostrae dignitate: sed una illi causa est beneplacitum aeternum, quo nos praedestinavit" (Calvin).[122] God loves us for his own sake. God himself constitutes the possibility that we become his children. God himself gives us this promise. In God himself and only in him is its fulfillment and reality to be found. Regarding this point, Calvin says: “Hic verus fons est unde haurienda est divinae misericordiae cognitio.”[123] He and his kin do not shake their heads, baffled and horrified at the possibility that everything—everything—could hang on the single thread of God’s will, or—we might as well go ahead and speak the horrible word out loud—the arbitrary act,[124] namely, God’s free election. For them, this knowledge alone affords knowledge of God’s saving mercy because it is founded on unshakable certainty, whereas they found in any allegedly reciprocal relation between God and man the element of uncertainty, which was unbearable for their faith.

Conversely, all domesticated piety, which regards *living* with God to be more important than living with *God*, finds this insight to be objectionable and relegates it to the background as much as possible. What becomes of us if, even for a second, we are separated from the *beneplacitum* of God? What becomes of our certainty if we lack the kind of certainty that God himself gives? How can we live with God when we can only believe in God? Any rapprochement between Pauline-Reformation piety and this domesticated-bourgeois piety is out of the question. Anyone who contends that the former is valid merely as a corrective and counterweight, and who wishes to raise the banner for a more practical form of piety, will find plenty of justification in history to do so. It is even more certain that Pauline logic is supported by the subject,[125] whereas the luxuriant vines of Pelagianism and Semipelagianism, otherwise known as church history, live fundamentally from *their* resources. One person considers the honor of God to be preeminent and waits for the salvation of man with the sole concern that God may receive the honor; another is concerned above all for man’s salvation and asks about the honor of God only for the sake of this goal. These two people will always talk past each other, and no formula of concord between them is possible. Here, κατὰ τὴν εὐδοκίαν τοῦ θελήματος αὐτοῦ is essential. Here, the recognition of what is beyond us is essential. Here, election is essential. It is a case of Either-Or!

And now finally: Where does the journey lead? What are God’s intentions in Christ? For what purpose does he determine that we should be his children through him? Answer: εἰς ἔπαινον δόξης τῆς χάριτος αὐτοῦ ἧς ἐχαρίτωσεν ἡμᾶς ἐν τῷ ἠγαπημένῳ. With that phrase, the first circle that Paul describes here is complete. It brings to mind the famous formula in Romans 11:36: ἐξ αὐτοῦ καὶ δι' αὐτοῦ καὶ εἰς αὐτὸν τὰ πάντα. God's purpose resides in himself. It is to glorify himself that he goes his wonderful way with us. Therefore, at each moment he necessarily has the last word and fills [?] the room [?]. For that reason, we never arrive at a point of stasis with regard to knowing, possessing, and enjoying what God has in mind for us. For the same reason, the divine reality that we encounter in Christ is merely [?] the crisis of everything human. Open your eyes and look. Open your ears and listen. The crisis is where our salvation is found. See and hear the good news of grace that is announced there. Because if God himself is the goal, then grace is his goal. Grace is his essence and is revealed to us only in Christ, when we come to the place where we seek God himself and him alone. Then he *speaks* with us. Then he *gives* himself to us. Then he *is* our God, our *Father*. Is this true? we ask. Can a person be led to the place where he seeks only God himself and him alone? What distinguishes the tidings of despair from the tidings of grace? What gives man the right to say, "If I have only you, I ask for nothing in heaven or earth" [Ps. 73:25]? How does God's freedom become our freedom and his goal, which is himself? How does it become our salvation? Paul answers: by the grace with which God has graced us in the Beloved. The election of our existence as the elect exists in Christ. The determination of God concerning us is love. The *beneplacitum* of God is his good pleasure to us. Here the mystery is revealed. Why? Because precisely here God comes as *word* on the cross of Christ but becomes word as *God* in his resurrection.

*Jan. 19, 1922*

Verses 7–14 describe the blessings with which God has blessed us—now from the vantage point of the *present*. The discussion moves from the distant past—πρὸ καταβολῆς κόσμου, when God elected us to be his children, in love, according to the good pleasure of *his* will to praise the glory of *his* grace—to seemingly more familiar territory. With the expression ἔχομεν (v. 7), our feet touch the familiar ground of human being, having, and doing, where we can catch our breath for a moment. We should be careful not to exaggerate the advantages of this vantage point. Even a superficial view of these verses reveals that they are speaking not about a *different* subject matter but rather about the *same* subject matter, only *differently*. Differently *because* the only method for speaking properly about *this* subject matter—if we can speak about a method at all—is to find ever new ways to speak about it. Therefore to speak properly about this subject matter is to recognize that all of our attempts to see and to speak about it are provisional so that our attention is drawn to—I am tempted to say "forced upon"—the object being considered and the content of what is written.

Paul deploys this method admirably. In verses 4–6 he speaks about the *past*, but what does the past mean if it refers to that which is eternally ordained for us in Jesus Christ? Clearly this past could just as easily be the present or the future. And now in verses 7–10 he *speaks* in fact about the present, but what does the present mean if it refers to the possession of our redemption, described here specifically as the knowledge of the mystery of God's will? Is it not clear that this present could just as easily be the past or the future? Our familiar human being, having, and doing are called into question from beyond just as bracingly in this second iteration, even though it is introduced by the apparently straightforward ἔχομεν. If we are prepared to hear what is truly being said here, then we cannot relax in this apparently more familiar territory; rather, the ἔχομεν points us back to the time frame of the past, which we just considered, or to yet a third temporal framework, that of the future, as Paul clearly does in verses 11–14, where he says the same thing once more by means of this third framework. By this juxtaposition, Paul makes it clear that his concern is not the past, present, and future as such, the καιροί (v. 10), which he regards as merely temporal frameworks, but the πλήρωμα τῶν καιρῶν, the *end* of time, eternity, which we can never speak about except by means of the temporal forms of the καιροί—yet paradoxically by continually altering and suspending these temporal dimensions. Our attention is diverted from the human observer and riveted upon that which is observed only when we recognize that we cannot speak about it unambiguously. The fact that we recognize the limitations of our discourse guarantees that we are speaking properly. Paul speaks about the ἔσχατον, speaks eschatologically, whether describing something that begins πρὸ καταβολῆς κόσμου or not, whether he is describing what *we have* or the inheritance for which *we hope*. How strange all of this sounds to us! The very strangeness of what Paul is saying accounts for its unambiguous clarity. The very fact that it eludes *our* grasp is evidence that *God* is being spoken about.

We "have" τὴν ἀπολύτρωσιν διὰ τοῦ αἵματος αὐτοῦ, τὴν ἄφεσιν τῶν παραπτωμάτων, κατὰ τὸ πλοῦτος τῆς χάριτος αὐτοῦ.

Ἀπολύτρωσις means the purchase of freedom. Human creatures are in prison; they have become slaves. They are set free from this slavery through a payment made on their behalf. What kind of slavery is this, and what kind of payment? Paul does not go into detail here. We learn only this much from the additional appositional clause: the slavery of humans is related to their sins; their sins have either landed them in prison or constitute the prisons themselves. Their manumission is essentially the forgiveness of their sins; they are no longer bound but released, just as a prisoner's chains are removed when he is granted freedom.

Paul regards man's state as a contradiction of the sonship for which he is eternally ordained. He is under a spell. He is living under tyranny. His own actions, his παραπτώματα, his trespasses, are the explanation for this state; and it amounts to the same thing if we say that the actions themselves constitute the bondage, the chains which hold him. This tyranny is absolute: rebellion or escape are both out of the question. Anything that the creature can do will simply perpetuate his own παραπτώματα, forge additional chains, deepen his bondage, and prolong his servitude. We are the guards of our own prisons; how could we possibly set ourselves free? For that, an ἄφεσις is needed. The command *Halt!* directed to us and our actions must come from beyond us. God must stand opposite the creature in order to say to him, *I* am your Lord! [cf. Exod. 20:2ff.; Deut. 5:6ff.], in order to set him free from himself. Man must face up to this claim on his existence so that he is compelled, awestruck, and totally absorbed by it. That is the forgiveness of sins. The good news of the forgiveness of sins means: we have received a new Lord! Whether we call the old lord "sin," *peccatum originale*, about which later church doctrine spoke so profoundly, or the "I" whom we know through our own experience, or the devil, what matters is that the Lord has become our Lord—absolutely. He has brought to an end the former tyranny. God is now our Lord. And he is our Lord in an absolutely different way than the sin that dominates us, because he is God. Slavery to sin is a breach of our freedom. We belong to the one who redeems us and claims what is justifiably—by a twofold right—his right as our creator *and* as our redeemer.

Suffice it to say that the forgiveness of sins is nothing less than God's rule. Forgiveness is by no means the only way to conceive of the rule of God, and it would be wrong to emphasize this motif alone to the exclusion of others. Forgiveness is not a matter of merely excusing a person; the one who is forgiven is also made obedient. The rule of God does not refer only to the dynamics of God's action; God's acquittal effects a corresponding dynamic in the creature, whose action is completely dissolved, reconstituted, and established on a new foundation. The word βασιλεία designates God's word as *act*. The terms ἄφεσις and ἀπολύτρωσις indicate God's act as nothing other than his *word*.

In addition to the appositional phrase τὴν ἄφεσιν . . . , Paul further clarifies ἀπολύτρωσις by saying [that it is] τὴν ἀπολύτρωσιν διὰ τοῦ αἵματος αὐτοῦ. The identity of the ἀυτός is clear from the conclusion of verse 6: he is the ἠγαπημένος, the one through whom God has graced us. By his blood we have the purchase of our freedom, our release from sin. When the New Testament refers to the blood of Christ, it means the suffering that Jesus endured in his passion, where the acquittal of man is announced by God, albeit in obscurity and hiddenness. The *Halt!* confronting our action and the total claim of our new Lord, who is actually our original Lord, is proclaimed. Διὰ τοῦ αἵματος αὐτοῦ or ἐν τῷ αὐτοῦ αἵματι (Rom. 3:25), Jesus is the ἱλαστήριον . . . , the *Kapporeth* of the Old Testament ark of the covenant, the place where on the Day of Atonement peace between God and his people was proclaimed by the sprinkling of blood [cf. Exod. 25:16–17; Lev. 16:14]; consequently, Jesus is the place of propitiation, where our lot turns, where we exchange masters, and where our sins are forgiven.[126]

The truth of this pronouncement—that God intends to be our God and Father through Jesus—is actualized only when God himself announces it, continually, that is, in our present situation, through the Spirit. How could we understand the meaning of the blood of Jesus, of his suffering and action in the passion, apart from the resurrection, which reveals their meaning? The resurrection in turn is revealed to us only through the cross and blood of Jesus. And so the cross simultaneously reveals what is seen and veils what is unseen. The ἀπολύτρωσις, the ἄφεσις, occurs here as *God's* mystery and act: *here* because it is precisely here, where all light is extinguished and the darkness of Golgotha enfolds even God's Son, that God *alone* can be seen to speak, act, and reveal himself. Let us be clear about what we mean when we say with Paul: ἔχομεν τὴν ἀπολύτρωσιν. We are saying that we have what only God has, what we [can] have only in God, who unites time and eternity. In other words, we have what we must receive continuously from God in each present moment.

I am familiar with the attempts of so-called Biblical Realism, which is not content with redemption on these terms but attempts to advance beyond the Reformation doctrine of justification to what it claims is a more robust and living fellowship with God. In fact, this approach is simply a form of naturalism. I confess that in the past, I was influenced by J. T. Beck's ideas. I abandoned this approach, however, because I became convinced that its gains in concreteness and vividness come at the expense of actual content. I judge any religious concept by the degree to which it makes me truly attentive to God himself, by the degree to which it witnesses to the reality that cannot be grasped by any religious concept. That quality clearly seems to diminish the more we assume that the parable coincides with the subject matter, and this is clearly the tendency of Biblical Realism.

An excellent example is Beck's interpretation of this very passage, especially the phrase διὰ τοῦ αἵματος αὐτοῦ. He speaks about the "sanctified and sanctifying life force of Christ's soul,"[127] which has been transformed into his nature and particularly into his blood. By this account, blood is no longer a material substance but the animating element of Jesus's body. By virtue of this purifying, sanctifying dynamic,[128] the blood of Jesus Christ now has purifying and sanctifying effects in the bodily-spiritual spheres, whose concrete substance is the blood itself. Through his Spirit, the sanctifying effects of his blood extend to all who are purified with him. Granted, that is certainly realism; but if I had to give it a name, I would call it not "biblical" but "mystical-theosophical realism." And I reject such approaches because, like all mysticism and theosophy, they attempt to avoid the offense of the cross and the necessity of faith. The word of God does not become more real by being refashioned into human reality. We should be content with its own reality rather than trying to make it conform to ours through such attempts. Let us be content with *that* ἔχομεν, which takes *our* breath away, because that is how God breathes *his* breath into us [cf. Gen. 2:7; Ps. 104:30].

The third phrase, κατὰ τὸ πλοῦτος τῆς χάριτος αὐτοῦ, clearly points us in this direction. It defines ἔχομεν the same way that the phrase ἧς ἐπερίσσευσεν defines our human being and having. We have liberation, the forgiveness of sins. But how do we have it? To avoid any misunderstanding, God alone must receive the honor: we have it "in accordance with the riches of his grace." God's grace is so much richer than we can conceive or imagine that his light illuminates our darkness: in that place where we can detect only the triumph of sin, where even the Son of God is accounted as sinful and allows himself to be so reckoned, precisely there, God's grace and truth triumph by his blood. His grace is that great, his truth that deep. No human parable is adequate for *this* reality. This reality signals *the* parable that is the end of all parables. Although we understand parables, we sigh and cry out with the disciples between Good Friday and Easter about the unreality that faces us in this parable, which is the parable of *death*. Even for Jesus, this was necessarily the final parable. Whoever is not afraid of this parable but sees the reality of God in light of it *has* ἀπολύτρωσις and ἄφεσις. And whoever does not fear but believes in light of it has *grace* and sees the Resurrected One. It goes without saying that this grace is not restricted to Easter morning. *His* grace, *God's* grace, is always present. Certainty is always found in *God*, and it is always *found* in God. How can we complain that the foundation of Christian ἔχομεν is grace alone when God himself makes it the basis of our certainty? I think that we would do better to part with our supposed attempts at clarity and be content with God's clarity.

Concerning this grace of God that is turned to us by Jesus's blood, the text adds: ἧς ἐπερίσσευσεν εἰς ἡμᾶς ἐν πάσῃ σοφίᾳ καὶ φρονήσει. This phrase forms the transition to γνωρίσας ἡμῖν, which in turn introduces the second sentence in which Paul describes what we have. The phrase beginning with γνωρίσας is the exact parallel to the sentence that begins with προορίσας in verses 5–6. This strongly suggests that γνωρίσας in verse 9 goes with ἐν πάσῃ σοφίᾳ καὶ φρονήσει, designating the wisdom and insight of God,[129] just as γνωρίσας is connected to ἐν ἀγάπῃ in the earlier sentence. So argues Beck.[130] In fact, the context does not provide evidence for this connection: it is not the wisdom and insight that effects God's revelation but his revelation itself that is praised and for which we are to be thankful. Σοφία and φρόνησις actualize our deliverance. Σοφία means insight into the last things, into God's ultimate purpose—the knowledge of God, in other words. Φρόνησις refers to the ultimate insight into penultimate realities, things visible, and quotidian affairs. Such knowledge, which is lavished upon us as from an overflowing vessel, constitutes our deliverance and the riches of God's grace. Only knowledge? Is this the alleged intellectualism of Ephesians and of Paul? Only correct thinking? Only an idea? It is not much, but then what else could we have? A feeling? Volition? Σοφία and φρόνησις identify the crisis in which we stand. Therefore, the adjective "only" is completely out of place here. God's idea constitutes our relation to God's reality. Knowledge of forgiveness is forgiveness.

*Jan. 25, 1922*

The overall parallelism between verses 4–6 and verses 7–10, and more specifically between προορίσας ἡμᾶς and γνωρίσας ἡμῖν, suggests that the latter phrase introduces a second description of the ideas expressed in the first set of verses. The relationship between the two clauses is governed by the relative clause in verse 8, ἧς ἐπερίσσευσεν. Inasmuch as we receive ἀπολύτρωσις and ἄφεσις, the abundance of God's grace is lavished upon us. How? As perfect wisdom and insight: we know how things stand with both eternal and penultimate matters. That knowledge constitutes our present ἔχομεν, our εὐλογία πνευματική in the present. Paul says that ἔχειν τὴν ἀπολύτρωσιν, τὴν ἄφεσιν is synonymous with the receiving of γνῶσις, the knowledge of the will of God. We have deliverance and forgiveness because God is present with us in the one who γνωρίσας τὸ μυστήριον τοῦ θελήματος αὐτοῦ.

As I said at the conclusion of the previous lecture, it is completely unjustified to accuse Paul of intellectualism or to reject the obvious meaning of this passage because of an anti-intellectual bias. Γνῶσις, knowledge of the will of God—or to express it objectively, γνωρίζειν, God's revelation of his eternal will—cannot be dismissed or qualified by the adjective "only" when referring to the Pauline gnosis. The Pauline concept of γνῶσις is every bit as dynamic and robust as the Lutheran concept of faith; it is as *all-encompassing* and grounded just as absolutely in the *reality* of God. Γνῶσις in this later Pauline letter has the pride of place occupied by πίστις in the major letters. Presumably Paul made this change because he needed to *intensify* what he had expressed with the word πίστις; that is, he needed to *express more emphatically* the object of faith, or rather, the origin of the relationship that he describes. Evidently, the term πίστις lost the ring of objectivity with Paul's later congregations that it had for the apostle. Despite his preference for the former term—and here he exemplifies the undogmatic dogmatician—he substituted the latter, which was bound to remind them that *God* is the A and the Ω of faith [cf. Rev. 1:8]. When one speaks about the *knowledge* of God, the emphasis is on God *confronting* us as the wholly *Other*. By contrast, πίστις implies that God confronts us while remaining in relation to us; this relational dimension—that we are his and he is ours—is not excluded but rather included if we say that God *reveals* himself and that we *recognize* him. Granted, when we describe man's relationship with God as γνῶσις, we enter a danger zone where "intellectualism" lurks at the door, as demonstrated by developments in the second century. But every human activity, particularly theological activity, is a matter of escaping one danger after the next. No *single* term assures unmistakable clarity. Everything in its own time [cf. Eccles. 3:1], πίστις *and* γνῶσις. For the sake of the subject matter, freedom, and comprehensiveness, we should be prepared to sacrifice or adapt our terms—even our favorite terms—if they contribute to misunderstanding. A theologian must be able to speak occasionally as a thoroughgoing gnostic. So much for the γνῶσις ἡμῖν, which rather surprisingly is a synonym for ἔχομεν τὴν ἀπολύτρωσιν.

The subject matter of this revelation is τὸ μυστήριον τοῦ θελήματος αὐτοῦ. Mystery according to Paul is not only God's hiddenness in general. For Paul, there is mystery whenever God's purpose and ways are veiled, as if a curtain obscures the temporal, concrete reality of all things human. There is mystery whenever God is silent and we hear something else instead of God. This other, the reality of the world,[131] initially effects an absolute occlusion. Because of it, we cannot perceive the will of God. Whoever desires to know God's purpose directly on the basis of what is observable and concrete, whoever is offended by this mystery, will only be undone by it. Because our vision is occluded, an act of revelation is necessary. Every veil must be rent; all human reality must be upended. *God* must speak, and God must *speak*, if we are to understand his will. This is what Paul means when he refers to marriage as a mystery in Ephesians 5:32; or to the mystery of lawlessness that delays the dawn of Jesus Christ in 2 Thessalonians 2:7; or to the mystery of the coexistence of the living and the dead in 1 Corinthians 15:51 when speaking of the resurrection; or to the hardening and rejection of Israel in Romans 11:25. In our passage, it is the θέλημα of God that is veiled in mystery. God, however, has revealed the mystery and disclosed his will.

What exactly is this μυστήριον, before which God is initially silent and whose temporal reality initially hides his purpose from us? To answer this question, we must anticipate the main clause in verse 10: it is the paradoxical fact of the historicity of Christ, the eruption of eternity into time, the singularity of the divine inevitability.[132] The riddle before which Paul stands is the present moment, the now, the today, which he believes is coexistent with the name of Jesus. Is this name merely one name among many others? Is this moment merely one contingent event[133] in an endless series of moments? Could this present stand majestically *above* both the past and the future rather than being a fleeting in-between moment that immediately vanishes? Could the will of God exist as a unity in the scattered temporal existence of man? Could there be a present moment in which we are able to know this will, this unity, actually present to us personally and compellingly?

The meaning of our existence depends on the πλήρωμα τῶν καιρῶν, the fulfillment of time, the eternal dimension of time, which confronts us here and now. But even the will of God is enshrouded in mystery for us. Direct knowledge of his will is impossible, even unimaginable for us. Direct knowledge is by definition finite and temporal knowledge, even when it concerns Jesus. Even his "today" is marked by contingency. Even his temporal existence in and of itself is unqualified.[134] Here too we face the aforementioned question about the will of God and of the unity of all things. How could it be otherwise? How do we come to Jesus the *Christ*? How and why is it possible to encounter the eternal here? And how and why here exactly? The μυστήριον and silence of God also apply to the historicity, contemporaneity, and uniqueness of the historical moment. Anyone who is not frightened by God's silence in the present or can never be frightened by it will not recognize it when God breaks the silence and *speaks*, when temporal reality becomes the theater for the decisive, divine word in its eternal mystery. Γνωρίσας ἡμῖν. Jesus *is* the Christ. The πλήρωμα τῶν καιρῶν, the eternal present, *appears* in the unobservable midpoint between past and present. The will of God *meets* us. The *disiecta membra*[135] of this world-reality *do have* a unity. This is so because of *God's* reality, *God's* act, *God's* revelation. *The* moment that so qualifies it is *God's* truth, *God's* act, *God's* revelation and not the moment in and of itself. It is not the threshold between just *any* past and *any* future. It completely separates *the* past from *the* future: *the* past is all time from the very beginning to the remotest future; *the* future is eternity. In him, a *single* moment reveals what the many fluctuating moments *point* to but are not in themselves.

Think about Selma Lagerlöf's legend about Christ in which two pillars, which have stood side by side since primeval times, move apart, allowing the twelve-year-old Jesus to enter.[136] So it is when the will of God meets us. There, between yesterday and today, dawns an incomparable today. There, time is split. There, world-reality is not destroyed but turned upside down. There, God reveals his mystery. This-world reality—that is, anything temporal, historic, or contingent—remains God's *mystery*, which he must reveal so that we understand it as the mystery of *God*. And he does reveal it. The liberation of man (ἀπολύτρωσις) and the forgiveness of sins constitute the revelation of his mystery. The phrases "through his blood" and "according to the riches of his grace" make it clear that the ἔχειν of verse 7 designates *the* unique having, which we have in God alone, and amounts to *our* not having. Who really *has* the resurrection? Who really *has* grace? Who could possibly boast that he has God in the fullness of his reality? That is the point. Anything less than resurrection, less than grace, less than God's reality, does not qualify as ἀπολύτρωσις and as ἄφεσις τῶν παραπτωμάτων. That is the meaning of this ἔχειν, according to verse 9. God has *revealed* his reality to us. That says it all—neither too much nor too little. We know God—as the *unknown* God. To think of God is to confront the mystery of God—the revealed mystery. The one interprets and clarifies the other and would not be true without the other. The Christian gnostic who is concerned with the reality of God as the forgiveness of sin is a Socratic in the strictest sense: he knows that he knows nothing. But precisely in his lack of knowledge, in his *humilitas* before God, which Calvin knew and spoke about so often, he is the one who truly knows and has overcome ἀγνωσία τοῦ θεοῦ (1 Cor. 15:34).

I am indebted to Haupt for my reading of verses 9–10; his commentary is the most reliable guide to the difficulties in this passage. Accordingly, I place *a dash after* αὐτοῦ: the will of God consists in bringing together all things in Christ according to his good pleasure. And I place *a parenthesis around the phrase that begins with* ἣν and ends in καιρῶν: God's good pleasure refers to the οἰκονομία, the creation and orchestration of the πλήρωμα τῶν καιρῶν.*

Let us consider first the central motif: ἀνακεφαλαιώσασθαι τὰ πάντα ἐν τῷ Χριστῷ. The accomplishment of this ἀνακεφαλαιώσασθαι according to his sovereign purpose and his *beneplacitum* is the will of God, which is hidden from us and known exclusively through revelation. Inasmuch as God reveals his will to us, we receive liberation and forgiveness. Furthermore, he reveals his will to us by the blood of Christ, according to the riches of his grace, as we learn from verse 7. To understand this ἀνακεφαλαιώσασθαι as the will of God is to have the understanding that *surpasses* all understanding. The term

*The editor of the German edition comments, "Keine logisch-sachliche Abfürung, sondern Parallelen"—literally, "Not logical-material removal, but parallel."

ἀνακεφαλαιώσασθαι refers to a thought process;[137] that is, the actual reality and occurrence of the will of God lies beyond the conception itself. Understanding the will of God does not mean direct knowledge of its fulfillment. We see God's plan, God's course. We have reason to hope. We know that there is something to believe in. However, faith and hope are just as necessary after understanding God's will as before. The paradox of the human situation is continually present and must be continually overcome. We know the will of God, the truth of which is revealed beyond the paradox, only when we wait upon the Lord as his servants, only when we are content to know our Lord's thoughts, even if they are only thoughts. Ἀνακεφαλαιώσασθαι means to gather together and integrate diverse elements. To use a mathematical expression, it is to reduce a series of numbers to their common denominator. That unity is God's conception and will. The assumption is that this conception has not yet become a reality. The world, τὰ πάντα, is fragmented into a multitude of particulars. Its essence is disintegration, fragmentation, dissolution, isolation, and complete contradiction between competing entities, all claiming to be ultimately true. As on earth, in the known, observable world, so it is in the heavenly realm, which is hidden from us. We cannot think God's thoughts without remembering the antithesis between the creator and creation, without recalling the dissolution of all finite things. Any unity that can conceive or create remains merely finite, temporal, and relative, pointing beyond itself to an antithesis. Ultimately, any human ἀνακεφαλαιώσασθαι is an illusion. The idea of unity—the unity of this world with the next, God with humanity, eternity with time—is God's conception and therefore humanly inconceivable. He and he alone can create such a unity. He and he alone is the Lord over life and death [cf. Rom. 14:9]. He *is* this unity, and this unity is his will. In him it *is* already at hand. In Christ we can and should know this unity. And precisely this knowledge is our liberation, the forgiveness of sins. Here, there appears a reality beyond our imprisonment, a real beyond.

Ἣν προέθετο ἐν αὐτῷ εἰς οἰκονομίαν τοῦ πληρώματος τῶν καιρῶν. This phrase provides a parallel explanation. The present *emptiness* described in this phrase corresponds to the fragmentation in the previous phrase. *Fulfillment* refers to the aforementioned summing up and gathering together. In Christ all time is fulfilled. God's present contains the fulfillment *of all* time. To achieve this fullness, to manage the household, so to speak, is God's purpose. Now we who live in time are able to see in the light of eternity.

*Feb. 2, 1922*

I have an additional observation about verse 10. The phrase τὰ ἐπὶ τοῖς οὐρανοῖς καὶ τὰ ἐπὶ τῆς γῆς is in apposition to τὰ πάντα. Therefore, the phrases ἐπὶ τοῖς οὐρανοῖς and ἐπὶ τῆς γῆς refer to the place or location where the objects, creatures, or essences designated by τὰ πάντα are found. The synthesis, the ἀνακεφαλαιοῦν, identified as the will of God in verses 9–10, spans both heaven and earth. So the text is not describing the reconciliation of the heavenly spheres with the terrestrial spheres *below* or peace between heaven and earth, between angels and humanity; rather, it describes the reconciliation of everything—including the conflicting world orders, the heavenly and the terrestrial realms, all that is in them—with *God* and by the will of God, who is the source of their unity. Because of the deliverance, the fullness of time that God wills—in the previous lecture I pointed out how Paul regards everything that exists as a series of concentric circles—definitely *extends* to the metaphysical landscape, whose existence Paul clearly acknowledged. Whatever else we might say about heaven and its inhabitants, about angels and spirits, the reconciliation is not between οὐρανοί, as the ultimate reality, and earth; rather, it is the reconciliation of the will of God with both *heaven* and earth, the physical and the *metaphysical*.

Our passage is saying that the most diametrically opposed antitheses that we can imagine all stand as numerators in relation to God, their *single* common denominator. There is no suggestion here of physical-cosmic deliverance. Anything that we consider "otherworldly" is really no more than an extension or an enhancement of this world, a replication of its contents, all of which are sorely in need of the divine ἀνακεφαλαίωσις. "Quae enim proportio creaturae ad creatorem, nisi intercedat mediator?"[138] asks Calvin in reference to the angelic world. Any deliverance whose consummation is *this* humanly conceived beyond—whether *we* go to this heaven or *this* heaven comes to earth—would be no deliverance at all. The *actual* beyond is God alone.* What the text describes is the *actual* beyond: the will of God, which is the unity of *heavenly* and terrestrial things, of what we call "this world" *and* of what we call "beyond."

This *beyond*, which surpasses both worldly and otherworldly spheres, is emphasized once more at the end of the verse by ἐν αὐτῷ. The phrase is part of the preceding clause and should not be joined to the clause that follows (contra Nestle).[139] If they were so joined, they would form an anacoluthon or an unexpected repetition of the ἐν ᾧ, which is possible given the awkward style of this passage. However, the parallelism that we have observed between verses 4–6 and verses 7–10 brings to mind the ἐν τῷ ἠγαπημένῳ at the end of verse 6; correspondingly, ἐν αὐτῷ is the conclusion of the phrases that immediately precede it. Here, ἐν αὐτῷ refers to Christ the same way that ἐν τῷ ἠγαπημένῳ does in verse 6 (in contrast to the ἐν αὐτῷ in verse 11).[140] *That* is the will of God: to join together all things in Christ, both the heavenly and the terrestrial things in him. The reference to Christ is a device that Paul uses to focus the attention and to demonstrate how heaven and earth, immanence and transcendence, are encompassed by the will of God. Conversely, he maintains that this radical ἀνακεφαλαίωσις, this drastic relativization of heaven and earth, takes place through Christ. Now it is clear why he can equate [this ἀνακεφαλαίωσις] with both the forgiveness of sins and the fulfillment of time: he regards all three as equally valid instantiations of the divine act of revelation, which calls everything into question and redeems all that is questionable. Precisely where Christ dwells among these unimaginable regions according to Paul is impossible to say on the basis of this passage. In any case, whenever we have a hard time understanding Paul, we should note that all the difficulties of his message can be reduced to *one* point. He presents us with a riddle—not *many* but *one*. And he *insists* on posing exactly the same riddle again and again. The riddle and its answer are one and the same.

We now consider the third circle of the prologue, verses 11–14, which describes the εὐλογία πνευματική of verse 3 from the perspective

*At this point in the margin of the manuscript, Barth penciled in a diagram with these words: "God! and earth, heaven, this world, the world beyond, physics, metaphysics."

of the *future*, now under the rubric of hope. This is undoubtedly Paul's intention, given the prominence of προηλπικότας in the first half of the paragraph and ἐν τῷ Χριστῷ ἐσφραγίσθητε τῷ πνεύματι τῆς ἐπαγγελίας in the second. Notice the dialectical subtlety with which Paul accomplishes his aim. Given what he says in verse 7, we must ask: What exactly is this future, if it is God's future and the future that we already have, albeit only as future?[141] Couldn't *this* future just as easily be called "past" or "present"? And in fact, as the concepts of υἱοθεσία and χάρις, which describe relationships in the *present*, stood at the midpoint of verses 4–6; and as the *eschatological* terms "forgiveness of sins," "the fulfillment of time," and ἀνακεφαλαίωσις stood at the midpoint of verses 7–10; so now at the midpoint of verses 11–14 stand, paradoxically, not a future being and having but rather the aorists ἐκληρώθημεν and ἐσφραγίσθητε because of the theme of election in verse 11. Understandably, many interpreters completely overlook the transition that occurs between verses 10 and 11 and regard the ensuing verses as simply a continuation of the theme of Christian salvation in the present. The transition is evident, however, if we note the material *meaning* of those aorists and what they say about the nature of the Christian's existence. In contrast to verses 7–10, which describe Christians as those who are ordained to wait, this section describes them as those who are ordained to hope.[142] We must pay attention to these intratextual connections in order to do justice to the content of the prologue, even though they do not qualify as "commentary" in the usual sense.

The paragraph begins with the aorist passive ἐκληρώθημεν, emphasized by καί. There are three possible ways to translate κληροῦσθαι: "were redeemed" (Hofmann),[143] "have received an inheritance or property" (Beck);[144] or "to share in the inheritance" (Meyer and the more recent commentators).[145] Because verse 14 refers explicitly to κληρονομία ἡμῶν, I prefer the third option, but either of the other two are valid translations. Because we are in him, in Christ, we have reason to hope for an inheritance. The blessing that has been promised to us in Christ is the hope that, though we live in this world, we are headed for the world to come. We look forward to all the benefits that come *from there*, and from there we expect *every* possible good. Notice how ἔχομεν in verse 7 takes on new meaning viewed from this angle. Clearly, Christians possess something; they possess hope. Is that all? Yes, that is all. There is nothing else in addition to that. But then, what could we have or hope for that is greater than living hope in an inheritance that includes *everything*?

As those who hope and wait, Paul adds parenthetically, we are προορισθέντες κατὰ πρόθεσιν τοῦ τὰ πάντα ἐνεργοῦντος κατὰ τὴν βουλὴν τοῦ θελήματος αὐτοῦ. There are two threats to the believer's hold upon hope: (1) We can mistake our own human hopes for *the* one great hope in the blessing of the redemptive future of God. We all have these hopes—it is inevitable. But through the demonic element that accompanies these human hopes, the all-consuming eschatological expectation can be lost. (2) Christian hope is unseen [cf. Rom. 8:24–25]. We are not given an indubitable pledge of its fulfillment, the type of pledge that would make faith superfluous—even for a moment. The very Spirit who is the pledge of our inheritance, according to verse 14, is the Spirit of promise. The prototype of the Christian who lives in hope will always be Abraham, who believes παρ' ἐλπίδα ἐπ' ἐλπίδι (Rom. 4:18).

How can we maintain our grasp upon hope in the face of these threats? Paul addresses the twofold threat of human *arrogance* and human *faintheartedness* by reminding us of our election, by the constant reminder that our existence in Christ is from *God* alone. Even our grasp upon hope is not up to us. Our claim on our eternal inheritance is not subject to the ebb and flow of the demonic element of our passions. Hope's all-consuming eschatological expectation is assured independently of our fluctuating passions, which are "Sky high exulting / To death burdened down."[146] As an heir of the world to come, the Christian is *sui juris*, or rather *divini juris*.[147] His fellowship with God comes with unassailable certainty because he has it like he has nothing else. It is real certainty precisely because it depends on God and not on himself. He is προορισθείς, ordained and chosen for election by God, a priori from eternity.

Paul expresses this thought in two parallel phrases with κατά. The believer is ordained and chosen for election, first, according to the purpose of the one who ἐνεργεῖ τὰ πάντα and has power over all things. This is the assurance in the face of human faintheartedness: there is no reason to lament the fact that we must believe *without* seeing, because the invisible God in whom we believe is the creator of all things visible. And, second, according to God's will, for the accomplishing of his purpose—which is the meaning of βουλή. This is the safeguard against human arrogance. It is God, and not we ourselves, who has made us his people and the sheep of his pasture [cf. Ps. 100:3]. We should never fall into the trap of thinking that our hope is or ever will be *our* hope. Our hope is founded on a foundation that is far more substantial than anything we can create for ourselves because it comes from God.

What is the significance of such an assured Christian hope? Answer: we are κληρονόμοι εἰς τὸ εἶναι ἡμᾶς εἰς ἔπαινον δόξης αὐτοῦ τοὺς προηλπικότας ἐν τῷ Χριστῷ. The construction εἰς τὸ εἶναι harkens back to verse 4. Once again, Paul answers the question about the state of the person to whom God devotes himself and about God's designs for such a person: here, as the God who makes promises—in the previous passage, as the God who elects. And each *answer* clarifies the other: to hope in Christ *is* to be ἅγιοι καὶ ἄμωμοι before God; and to be holy and blameless before *God* is to hope in Christ. *This* is God's purpose for us in this world. *This* is his absolute claim on us: that we praise his glory, which is possible in our creaturely existence if we dare to *hope* in his word of promise. To hope is to intentionally align oneself with God, with all the risk that such partisanship involves. It is a declaration of war against the reality of this world.[148] You could call it the willingness to see the world completely unromantically and without any illusions.

The person who risks thinking the thought of eternity is precisely the person who can see time for what it is. He never mistakes time for eternity; and because he recognizes the difference, he has the courage to wait for eternity *in* time. Restrained yet completely free, taut yet nimble, the Christian praises the glory of God. All the demands of religion and ethics are included for him in the one simple requirement that he continually hope and wait. He is content to maintain a healthy skepticism. He doesn't get worked up about what he does not have yet because it is already there. And anything that is already present cannot be identified with Christ. Hope that is seen is not hope [Rom. 8:24]. The Christian remains content,* even childlike,

*The editor of the German edition adds "zu," which Barth omitted.

in the *very act* of waiting. He has the promise by virtue of *waiting* for it. Beck expresses it nicely: "Waiting on Christ's glorious future distinguishes true believers from all who seek glory in this age, even if they are seeking the glory of Christendom."[149] Notice especially the last part!

Bengel,[150] Meyer,[151] von Soden,[152] Dibelius,[153] and others regard προηλπικότας as a reference to the *Jewish* Christians, among whom Paul numbers himself by using the pronoun ἡμᾶς, subsequently distinguishing himself from gentile Christians by using the phrase ἐν ᾧ καὶ ὑμεῖς. There is superficial support for this position, including the change of the personal pronoun from ἡμᾶς to ὑμεῖς, the difficulty of coming up with an alternate meaning of προηλπικότες given the καὶ before ὑμεῖς (notwithstanding my alternate proposal, which follows), and the fact that the Jewish-Christian conflict figures prominently in Paul's other letters.

Nevertheless, I shall propose an alternative explanation for the reference to Jewish Christians. The change from ἡμᾶς to ὑμεῖς at the beginning of verse 13 more likely signals a rhetorical shift from general statements to direct address. The presence of καί in and of itself is inconclusive because ἐκληρώθημεν in verse 11 is also introduced with καί. In both instances and subsequently, καί before πιστεύσαντες has the effect of emphasizing the words that follow rather than signaling a contrast with what immediately precedes it. Moreover, as Beck points out, Paul normally uses the prefix προ- not to distinguish between various groups of people but to distinguish between God and man. In any event, we cannot overemphasize the difference between the Pauline προ- and any temporal beforehand. The beforehand of God is clearly nontemporal or beyond time—think, for example, about προγινώσκειν or προορίζειν—it is an antecedent that cannot be casually equated with any human antecedent. The προ- before ἠλπικότες is actually redundant, as Haupt correctly observes, here as in Romans 1:2, where Paul refers to the gospel as προεπαγγειλόμενον. In our passage, it clearly refers to the Christian's hope, which is grounded in God himself and therefore precedes and exceeds all hope, hope that is by its very nature assured, a priori. It is related to the προορισθέντες in the preceding verse and placed in the foreground by means of the all-important phrase ἐν τῷ Χριστῷ. Finally, the passage seems to me to be far too neutral to describe a conflict as sharp as the Jewish-Christian conflict and seems out of character with the overall style of the prologue.

So the phrase ἐν ᾧ καὶ ὑμεῖς in verse 13 does not, as I said, refer to gentile Christians as a distinct audience. If we have correctly interpreted the meaning of προηλπικότες, then it is clear that the "we" in verses 11–12 refers to the same subject as the "we" in the preceding paragraphs. Conversely, nothing is said about the "you" in ἐν ᾧ καὶ ὑμεῖς of verses 13–14 that does not apply equally to the "we" in verses 11–12. Therefore, I regard ἐν ᾧ καὶ ὑμεῖς as a rhetorical device. Paul concludes the prologue with an ad hominem argument, without excluding himself from his audience as a recipient of the spiritual blessing. After all, he is writing a letter, not a treatise. He is not speaking *about* Christians in general; he is addressing *these* particular Christians. And this is how he addresses them: You are those whom God appointed as κληρονόμοι so that you might dare to hope and therefore to live for his honor! You ἐσφραγίσθητε τῷ πνεύματι τῆς ἐπαγγελίας τῷ ἁγιῳ. And here, the train of thought moves from the participial phrases with ἀκούσαντες and πιστεύσαντες to the finite verb. The ἐσφραγίσθητε here is related to ἐκληρώθημεν in verse 11 in the same way that προορίσας in verse 5 is related to ἐξελέξατο in verse 4 and that γνωρίσας in verse 9 is related to ἔχομεν in verse 7.

In other words, this is a second description of the same reality, using different terms and images: Christians are those who wait for future glory. "Sealing" brings to mind a contract, which is legally valid by virtue of the seal that the contracting party places on the document. By virtue of the seal, the person vouches that he will honor the contract; so that seal serves as a guarantee in the person's absence, as effectively as if he were actually present. Christians have received such a seal from God—inasmuch as they are σφραγισθέντες, they have received the seal. The seal is the Holy Spirit of promise. It seems to me completely out of context to interpret this passage as a fulfillment of the Johannine promise of the Paraclete, that is, to suggest that they have the Spirit who was promised to them beforehand. No, the Spirit here is the *Spirit of promise*, as the word in the same verse is *the word of truth*. The word *is* the truth itself, and the Spirit *is* the promise itself. Whoever has the promise truly *has* it and the

Holy Spirit with it. The fact that the children of God wait for their inheritance, truly wait, is in itself the proof, guarantee, and surety that they do not wait in vain. God can vouch for his own promise, and the fact that God is with us as the pledge of his promise and personally witnesses to his own trustworthiness constitutes our sealing with the Holy Spirit. To have the Holy Spirit is to be content in God. Paul addresses the Christians in Ephesians on that basis: as those who are content in God and thereby feel that they are blessed by God. They are content with God's own trustworthiness [or veracity]. Perhaps this explains the real meaning of the phrase ἐν ᾧ καὶ ὑμεῖς: it is an appeal to the subjective in the reader, which in this case coincides with the objective.

The Spirit, previously identified by the phrase τῆς ἐπαγγελίας, is now described more precisely by the addition of the relative clause in verse 14: ὅ ἐστιν ἀρραβὼν τῆς κληρονομίας ἡμῶν εἰς ἀπολύτρωσιν τῆς περιποιήσεως. The word ἀρραβών, deposit or pledge, like ἀπαρχή elsewhere, implies that the possession of the Holy Spirit is not something to be enjoyed in and of itself. Rather, it is the guarantee of the eschatological future, the enjoyment of the kingdom of God. Hope is our endowment as Christians because we have our κληρονομία in *hope*. But in hope we actually *have* it—until we are admitted to the event described as ἀπολύτρωσιν τῆς περιποιήσεως, that is, until we come into our inheritance and gain access to what is ours. It is legitimate to equate this event with what is described in other Pauline passages as Christ's second coming in glory [cf. 1 Cor. 15:23–28; Phil. 3:20–21; 1 Thess. 1:10; 4:16]. It is the end, the outer limits of time, and the object of hope.

*Feb. 9, 1922*

We still need to consider the participial phrase in verse 13, ἀκούσαντες τὸν λόγον τῆς ἀληθείας, τὸ εὐαγγέλιον τῆς σωτηρίας ὑμῶν, and the phrase ἐν ὧ καὶ πιστεύσαντες, which accompanies and complements it. Both depend on the verb ἐσφραγίσθητε. God vouches for himself. God's promise is as certain as if it were already fulfilled because he is the one who makes the promise. This is so by virtue of the Holy Spirit. The future is already present for those who are sealed with the

Spirit, which is why Paul can speak about the future in terms of the present, as he does here. Their hope is not some private matter to be kept hidden; nor is it comparable to other hopes for the future, which are only relatively certain because they are subjective, conditional, and of relative importance. No, hope is secure, more secure and reliable than anything I might decide to do right now or what is about to happen in the next thirty seconds. It is not subject to anything contingent or relative, and it is certainly not a matter of religious enthusiasm. It is as likely to be expressed in the most prosaic of thoughts as it is in the most ecstatic utterances. It is always a factor and cannot for one moment be marginalized like so much of what passes for eschatology these days. No, ἔσχατον, properly understood, refers not only to the last things but also to the first and most important thing in each moment. This future shatters our concept of the future; or to be more precise, it reveals the limitations of our two-dimensional concept of the future. If you believe in the return of Christ, you necessarily acknowledge the *futurum aeternum*, which is the rehabilitation and renovation of *all* time, God's multidimensional present.

Paul addresses the Ephesian Christians as σφραγισθέντες. He applies the expression ad hominem—that is, he directs it to their subjectivity—by virtue of the phrase ἐν ᾧ καὶ ὑμεῖς. He *thereby* indicates *the precise point* where the objective εὐλογία πνευματική (v. 3) becomes subjective.[154] One *can* appeal to man's eternal hope. It is his great potential for relationship and communion, in whatever form or fashion. Is Paul wrong to assume that there is such a point in his listeners, that is, where the objective—their relation to God—coincides with their subjectivity? This perennial concern is addressed in the two participial phrases in verse 13. The point in us to which Paul refers is unassailable. It lies beyond the realm of matters that we either doubt or believe, accept or reject. Humanity and everything human is questionable. What is not in question is the relation of humanity and everything human to *God*. The more we recognize humanity's uncertainty, the more we recognize the certainty of man's relation to God. Indeed, the reason human existence in and of itself is dubious is precisely because humanity is originally related to God. Everything that is contingent and temporal is relative. What is not relative is the actual relation to the *Absolute*. The more clearly we recognize this relation for what it is, the more clearly we understand[155] the relativity of all things. And Paul addresses his readers here exactly on this basis: they really *have* this *insight*. They *have heard* the word of truth, the announcement of salvation. And more than that, they have *believed* (again, one should pay attention to the familiar καί). They have believed in him, in Christ. In Christ, the eternal hope of humanity has actually become the *presupposition* of humanity. Each moment in which we redirect our attention to him, we remember and are assured: we have heard; we have believed; we have understood; we have found the unassailable, immovable point. In him, the nongiven is given; God is revealed.[156] In him, the Spirit broods upon humanity, and God turns toward humanity in grace. In him, both the relativity of all things and their relation to the absolute are one. In him, one can hear what no ear has heard [cf. 1 Cor. 2:9] and can believe what is infinitely beyond belief. In him, God personally vouches to fulfill within the scope of human existence every promise he has made.

The λόγος τῆς ἀληθείας and the εὐαγγέλιον τῆς σωτηρίας refer to the advent of God's promise within human existence and our recognition of these promises. Both concepts must be understood analogically. It diminishes their significance to translate them thus: the word that "includes" or "brings" the truth, the gospel that "announces" salvation. No, the word *is* the truth (John 17:17), and the message of salvation *is* the δύναμις θεοῦ εἰς σωτηρίαν (Rom. 1:16). In both cases, the meaning of the genitive coincides with the meaning of the noun it modifies.[157] The message about salvation is so closely related to salvation itself that to hear and believe the word spoken in Christ is to hear and believe the truth directly. To be sure, the paradox remains: the truth about salvation comes in the form of hope, as sealing by the Spirit of promise. But it has been *given* to us. In Christ, a real *connection* between humans and the truth is established and remains; there is a real *expectation* of salvation—real in the sense that we already participate in the salvation that we anticipate.

Note the close, explicit connection between ἀλήθεια and σωτηρία. Salvation comes only from the truth. Whatever is not true—for example, millennial fervor that contradicts straightforward logic—cannot help us or save us either. And conversely, truth, real truth, is salvation. Whatever does not help us in the deepest sense, whatever fails to fundamentally transform the human condition, whatever remains in the realm of ideas alone, is also untrue. Questions about truth cannot be divorced from rational thought and concrete experience; ethics cannot be divorced from logic. The Holy Spirit is the promise of both: truth *and* salvation. This perspective calls into question our tidy distinctions between philosophy and theology. If it has merit, then a convergence of perspectives on the part of the two disciplines is the very least we should expect.

Εἰς ἔπαινον τῆς δόξης αὐτοῦ reappears at the end of verse 14 (cf. v. 6 and v. 12). It is governed not by the preceding phrase but by the finite verb ἐσφραγίσθητε, which, as Haupt correctly notes, is the crux of the sentence and the point to which the entire passage moves. Paul tells his readers that they are what they are—namely, blessed abundantly with the εὐλογία πνευματική—so that they may praise the glory of God. They have been charged with a great matter—indeed, the greatest matter. They are witnesses, heralds, deputies. The more fully they appropriate this blessing for themselves, the more fully the complete sweep of the blessing is revealed. Its truth comes from God and is found in God. Listen to what Calvin observes about this phrase, εἰς ἔπαινον τῆς δόξης αὐτοῦ, which appears repeatedly in our passage:

> Quod autem toties commemorationem gloriae Dei repetit, non debet videri supervacuum. Nam de re infinita nihil potest dici immodice. Praesertim valet hoc in commendanda Dei misericordia, cuius sensum quisquis vere pius erit nunquam poterit verbis aequare. Itaque tam narrandis eius encomiis promptas esse pias omnes linguas, quam aures libenter audiendis apertas esse convenit. Hoc enim argumentum est, in quo si totam suam facundiam explicent tam angeli quam homines, magnitudini tamen longe cedent.[158]
>
> (This frequent repetition and recollection of God's glory is by no means redundant because it is impossible to say too much about such an infinite matter. Especially in regard to God's mercy, no truly pious person would dream of exhausting its meaning with his own words. Precisely for this reason, pious lips must be just as eager to announce his praise as pious ears are willing to hear it. Therefore both men and angels remain debtors before this theme, even if they exhaust their wealth.)[159]

With that, we conclude our examination of the prologue. As we have seen, it is much more than an introduction. Bengel [called] it a "*compendium evangelicum*."[160] In any event, it is certainly a compendium of the Christian message in Ephesus and, most of all, a compendium of the fundamental Pauline framework. In one brief succession of sentences, it offers a glimpse into the unprecedented revolution that must have occurred in the hearts and minds of this group of people in the first century and the impression it must have made upon them—upon both Paul and his readers, whom he considered capable of understanding such ideas![161] It is impossible on the basis of historical analysis to perceive the essentially imperceptible event that occurred here, or anywhere for that matter, because the subject matter—like the essence of any such revolution, any such impression—eludes historical analysis, as can be shown by any number of parallel examples. However, I hope that I have convinced you that it is possible to enter sympathetically with Paul and not only to see along with Paul but to think along with him at that point where *the subject matter*, *the incommensurable*, *Jesus Christ*, speaks and becomes his own interpreter.[162] Since the passage affords such extraordinary possibilities for such a reading, I am surprised that it has not been more prominent in historic and systematic accounts of Christianity, and I hope that you are not disappointed that we have devoted the majority of the course to it.

# Ephesians 1:15–23

[15 Διὰ τοῦτο κἀγώ, ἀκούσας τὴν καθ' ὑμᾶς πίστιν ἐν τῷ κυρίῳ
Ἰησοῦ καὶ τὴν ἀγάπην τὴν εἰς πάντας τοὺς ἁγίους, 16 οὐ παύομαι
εὐχαριστῶν ὑπὲρ ὑμῶν μνείαν ποιούμενος ἐπὶ τῶν προσευχῶν
μου, 17 ἵνα ὁ θεὸς τοῦ κυρίου ἡμῶν Ἰησοῦ Χριστοῦ, ὁ πατὴρ τῆς
δόξης, δώῃ ὑμῖν πνεῦμα σοφίας καὶ ἀποκαλύψεως ἐν ἐπιγνώσει
αὐτοῦ, 18 πεφωτισμένους τοὺς ὀφθαλμοὺς τῆς καρδίας ὑμῶν,
εἰς τὸ εἰδέναι ὑμᾶς τίς ἐστιν ἡ ἐλπὶς τῆς κλήσεως αὐτοῦ, τίς ὁ
πλοῦτος τῆς δόξης τῆς κληρονομίας αὐτοῦ ἐν τοῖς ἁγίοις, 19 καὶ
τί τὸ ὑπερβάλλον μέγεθος τῆς δυνάμεως αὐτοῦ εἰς ἡμᾶς τοὺς πι-
στεύοντας κατὰ τὴν ἐνέργειαν τοῦ κράτους τῆς ἰσχύος αὐτοῦ 20 ἣν
ἐνήργηκεν ἐν τῷ Χριστῷ ἐγείρας αὐτὸν ἐκ νεκρῶν, καὶ καθίσας
ἐν δεξιᾷ αὐτοῦ ἐν τοῖς ἐπουρανίοις 21 ὑπεράνω πάσης ἀρχῆς καὶ
ἐξουσίας καὶ δυνάμεως καὶ κυριότητος καὶ παντὸς ὀνόματος ὀνο-
μαζομένου οὐ μόνον ἐν τῷ αἰῶνι τούτῳ ἀλλὰ καὶ ἐν τῷ μέλλοντι·
22 καὶ πάντα ὑπέταξεν ὑπὸ τοὺς πόδας αὐτοῦ, καὶ αὐτὸν ἔδωκεν
κεφαλὴν ὑπὲρ πάντα τῇ ἐκκλησίᾳ, 23 ἥτις ἐστὶν τὸ σῶμα αὐτοῦ,
τὸ πλήρωμα τοῦ τὰ πάντα ἐν πᾶσιν πληρουμένου.]

*15 Therefore, since I learned about your faith in the Lord Jesus and
your love for all the saints, 16 I have not stopped giving thanks for
you, remembering you in my prayers—17 that the God of our Lord
Jesus Christ, the Father of glory, may give you the Spirit of wisdom
and of revelation to know him, 18 the illumination of the eyes of your
heart so that you know what is the hope that is given to you through
his call, what is the abundance of the glory of his inheritance for his*

*saints, [19] and what is the surpassing greatness of his power for us who believe in the exercise of the power of his strength.*

*[20] He exercised this in Christ when he raised him from the dead and placed him at his right hand in the heavenly world: [21] over all origins and authorities and powers and dominions and over everything that can be named, not only in this world but also in the world to come; [22] and he placed everything at his feet and made him the head of everything in the church, [23] which is his body, the fullness of him who fills all in all.*

With the reminder of what has been given to Christians, Paul ends by letting his readers know that he prays for them, that what has already been given might be given to them afresh and even more abundantly. Because of God's blessing upon them, which he knows about from reports about them, he and they are bound together in community through God. For this reason, he prays for them continuously. The solidarity that unites them is not fortuitous but essential, not temporary but permanent. Once you have discovered *the* apex of life, which is εἰς ἔπαινον τῆς δόξης αὐτοῦ, you are reckoning with the bond that truly unites people, regardless of how tight or loose it may be in other respects.[163] Paul gives thanks for his readers—for all that they are and all that they have received—then immediately segues from thanksgiving to intercession (εὐχαριστῶν and μνείαν ποιούμενος occur in parallel!). If we look carefully at how he prays for them, it is striking that he does not pray for an increase of what they already have and already are. No, he goes right back to the beginning[164] and prays that they may have the Spirit and knowledge, as if he had not already explained at length they *are* Christians by virtue of how they have already been blessed. He does not take back or qualify anything he has said. It is not as if the blessing is incomplete. No, it is complete. It is given by God. Not a single thing is lacking. But as soon as he turns his attention to his readers and to himself, he reminds himself and them that he has been speaking about the blessing of *God*. As the blessing of *God*, it is completely new each new moment; its existence is not static. Indeed, nothing exists in and of itself[165]—"spiritualium bonorum satietate nihil periculosius" (Calvin).[166] There [where it is a matter of receiving God's blessing], *the human* creature stands before God empty-handed, poor, needy, and completely dependent upon *God*. There, he must pray. In the natural world, things simply grow. In the human realm, projects develop. In both cases, prayer does *not* come into consideration. Prayer *does* come into consideration, however, when the subject is our relation to God and to the εὐλογία πνευματική. For this blessing and this relation, we must return continually to the source and origin. This origin does not exist in the world or within time. Rather, the world, including time, is the veil, which conceals it. This veil must be *rent* repeatedly. The human creature must repeatedly *call upon* God as God.[167] Any truth that is *not new* does not qualify as God's truth. Likewise, when redemption ceases to be an object of hope and becomes something we possess or consume, it is no longer redemption. When the Spirit ceases to be the Spirit of promise and becomes something that we possess, even if it is our greatest possession, then it is no longer the Holy Spirit. That is the reason for this transition to intercession. Paul, the warrior for God,[168] emerges here. A new day has dawned. Yesterday's discovery must be sought anew today. Yesterday's rich are today's poor, and only as the poor will they become rich again. We have not reached the end of the pilgrimage; no goal or stage of an *ordo salutis*[169] has already happened; no presupposition for human existence is automatically predetermined. Here, we must confront the unvarnished truth anew in all of its complexity. Therefore, his prayer is: ἵνα ὁ θεὸς . . . δώῃ ὑμῖν. God must give all! The presupposition of the prayer and the prayer itself is that what is true may *become* true; that God's name, which is truly holy in itself, may *be hallowed*; that his eternal unchanging will may *be done*; that his kingdom, which is above all kingdoms, may *come* [cf. Matt. 6:9; Luke 11:2]. If we consider it redundant to pray for the hallowing of his name, the coming of his kingdom, and doing of his will—if we regard his name, kingdom, and will as no more than the evolution, extension, or continuation of what already exists—then obviously we do not know what we are saying when we say "God." And to know what we are saying when we say "God" can only be learned. Apart from this knowledge, we cannot pray. And we must pray in order to receive this knowledge.

This insight evokes Paul's prayer, and he prays that he and his readers may have this insight. Yesterday and today, riches and poverty, gaining or losing the one thing needful [cf. Luke 10:42] join as one in a dynamic movement that encompasses[170] the person when he discovers how he is related to God. And Paul prays for *the Spirit of wisdom and of revelation to know him*. He could not pray for them to receive the Spirit of wisdom and revelation if they did not already have it. But precisely because he does already have it and has complete confidence that his readers have it as well, he prays as if he did not have such a Spirit of wisdom and revelation. Σοφία refers to the divine dimension of the Spirit of wisdom and revelation; ἀποκάλυψις refers to same reality made accessible to us. Together, they constitute the knowledge of God.

"The enlightening of your eyes" is what he hopes for his readers. Apparently, Paul is using an expression that his readers would recognize from the mysticism of the period. And why not? The subject matter itself precludes any suggestion of new form of mysticism, even though he uses such vocabulary. Luther also traded on the mysticism of his time. Mystical thinking pervades Grünewald's *Isenheim Altarpiece*. There is no reason why God's truth could not be the focal point of mysticism, pagan or Christian. In any event, the mystic's vocabulary expresses exactly what Paul has in mind here: their inner eyes must be opened; they must be given eyes for what no eye has seen; they must perceive the imperceptible. By means of their God-given faith and love, which he praised earlier, they must look beyond what they already have in order to catch sight of the object of their faith.[171] Paul says this not as if they lack these eyes, this insight, and this capacity but equally not as if this possibility were somehow already realized. The realization of this possibility must always be the subject of prayer. Paul prays that they may *know* "the hope that is given to you through his call." They have received God's call. It constitutes their situation, their status, and their post—no more and no less. God's blessing is the great opportunity that has been given to them. Because of this opportunity, a new day has dawned. Presently, it remains an opportunity. They must grasp the ἐλπὶς τῆς κλήσεως, which comes with their position and recognizes their situation for what it is so that their opportunity may become a fruitful reality.

In the second half of verse 18 and in verse 19, Paul develops this idea on two fronts. He says, first, that they need to fully appreciate *what they may hope for*: the riches of the glory of his inheritance among his saints. In other words, it is essential to learn the *full extent* of what they can expect from God. Second, it is essential to notice how they *truly are permitted to hope for it* (v. 19), in other words, how fully they can *expect* what is promised. Paul uses such a profusion of phrases to express this hope that he nearly becomes tongue-tied: to hope in God is a mighty act, an act ordained by God. "When God creates faith in a person, it is a work that rivals the re-creation of heaven and earth. . . . Wherever God brings about faith, there is necessarily a new birth and a new creation" (Luther). *That* is the magnitude of the ἐνέργεια, the action of God that appears on the scene. Is that something that we already know? We know it on the basis of Christ's resurrection and ascent into heaven.

*Feb. 16, 1922*

Verses 20–21 are best understood as the answers to each of the questions that Paul poses in verses 18–19: *What* is the hope which you have been given (v. 18)? This first question is further developed in two subsequent questions in verses 18–19: *What* are the riches of his glorious inheritance among the saints? *What* is the surpassing greatness of his power for us who believe? Paul prays that his readers will have revelation and knowledge so that the eyes of their hearts will be opened that they will be able to understand and to hope and thereby to have an answer to this question: *What?* This for Paul is the heart of the matter and the enigma of their existence as Christians. What does it mean that we are blessed by God? What do we mean when we invoke God's name upon our existence as Paul does? What is given to those who have faith in the Lord Jesus and love for all the saints (v. 15)? What kind of power exerts its influence on Christians?

I have already pointed out how the same question appears at the end of 1 Corinthians, the well-known chapter on the resurrection, at the culmination of Paul's critically important controversy with the congregation in Corinth. The question of faith or doubt concerning the resurrection is not simply one religious or dogmatic question among others—that becomes clear in my opinion by the way Paul treats the matter in 1 Corinthians 15—rather, it is the question about the "*essence* of Christianity," to use the modern expression. This question about the essence of Christianity arises out of the question about the meaning of a believer's Christian existence. If we answer this question glibly or haphazardly, without proper regard for the historical distance, then we consider the essence of Christianity as amounting to its essential insignificance, to use Overbeck's expression.[172] Paul answers this question here, as in 1 Corinthians, by appealing to the *resurrection*. Indeed, he answers it by posing a new question—in fact, *the* new question. The more we emphasize the singularity of the question, the more accurately we represent what Paul is trying to say here. Glib or garrulous he certainly is *not*. Mouth-stopping would be more accurate—in the sense that he does not give what we consider to be an answer (any answer we can give to this question would definitely be glib). Rather, in the place of our penultimate question, he poses the ultimate question about the enigma of our existence in relation to God. If we see the answer *there*—in the *resurrection!*—in the *new question*, which is truly the *final*, *ultimate* question for us, then we understand the meaning of our Christian existence and the essence of Christianity as a historic phenomenon, according to Paul. In our passage, Paul gives the answer, or poses this new question, by means of three statements: (1) God raised Christ from the dead; (2) God has established him at his right hand; (3) God has made him head of the church. Such is the ἐνέργεια, the action of God and by analogy (κατά, v. 19) our own Christian existence. *That* is the meaning of the hope given to Christians by virtue of their calling. Paul prays that they may comprehend the meaning of their hope—as if comprehending it for the first time—because who is in a position to say that he already knows it?

When Paul speaks, first, *of the resurrection of Christ from the dead*, he means an event, but an event that is more nearly impossible and unhistorical than historical. He means the impossible event κατ' ἐξοχήν.[173] Let me put this even more precisely. Undoubtedly, Paul means an event, an occurrence. For Paul, the resurrection of Christ from the dead is an event occurring within history. It makes contact with what is possible, historic, and temporal; to that extent it is itself a historically possible and temporal event. He means an event that takes place precisely at the *boundary* between what is possible and what is impossible, what is historical and what is unhistorical, time and eternity. Eternity is related to time the way that the present exists between past and future because only the present is part of both time past and time in the future. And eternity is not in time, as present is not in time between past and future, because this time-constitutive point *is never* between past and future.[174] The resurrection of Christ from the dead is eternity. Eternity is God's present moment in time. Here, the answer is the *question*, and the question the *answer*.[175] Paul directs his readers' attention to this point in time as the basis of their Christian existence. Moreover, this point constitutes the essence of Christianity. Paul regards it as *given* in Jesus Christ. It is given in *history*, therefore not as something other than history, removed from history, in addition to history, or beyond history—not as a Platonic idea, as popularly conceived. It is given as an idea in the fullest sense, that is, as the idea or conception of *God*, therefore as the origin of all *origins*, the inaccessible in the immediate, the wholly other in the human, the beyond in *this life*. But note: it is given as an *event* in history, as *the other side* of this world, as an event that is in history but not *of* it—not a mere object of history but history's fundamental origin and absolute boundary. This boundary and origin are of a different order than anything that can be explained on *the basis of history* or examined within *the established order of knowledge*, even the most extraordinary and unprecedented event. For Paul and all of early Christianity, this point occurs *beyond* Jesus Christ's own history as well—namely, after his death.

The categories of *life* and *death* that Paul uses to describe this point in space and time are absolute categories, and I shall follow his lead. If Christ is in fact raised from the dead, then resurrection life is the new life of God himself, absolutely and categorically different from any other kind of life. If we think we understand it on the basis of human categories of knowledge, we can be sure that we have mistaken something else for the resurrection. To interpret it by human standards is to misinterpret it. Understandably, even early Christianity could only stutter when attempting to describe it. How could anyone find words for this *event*? Obviously, their attempts to describe it are contradictory and mutually exclusive. What human standard is adequate to measure *this* event? Subsequent attempts to conceive of this inconceivable occurrence have only proved how fundamentally inconceivable it is. The idea of finding the most plausible or convincing version from this welter of reconstructions is vain, in my estimation. Suppose we estimate the degree of accuracy of the most accurate reconstruction of the event, say the Pauline account, compared to others to be 1,000 to 1. Well then the degree of accuracy of even this most accurate reconstruction of the event, compared to the event itself, is 1,000 to infinity.[176] The reality is that the resurrected one appeared. The disciples *found* an answer to the forbidden [?] question on the other side of Good Friday. They encountered life where human eyes could detect only death. This is the absolutely implausible, improbable reality that must be reckoned with and that Paul did reckon with before its implausibility and improbability had been explained away and trivialized by appeal to experience. For Paul, there is no other plausibility and credibility than the plausibility and credibility of God.

The moment you speak about the revivifying of a body that was crucified and placed in a grave or about the appearance of the transfigured Lord, about a miracle and about a vision, you necessarily speak about *God*; and when you speak about God, the meaning of "miracle" and of "vision" are dissolved and reconstituted because the miracle that witnesses to God's reality is not one miracle among many but *the* miracle, nonpareil. The vision or perception of God is not one among others but *the* unique, incomparable vision. In any event, anyone who wants to account for this reality by appeal to experience should proceed with caution. The reality that Paul describes here is not experienced the way we experience anything else. It would be far more faithful to Paul to say that we do not experience it at all.

We should welcome the fact that historical-critical research reveals the contradictions among the various accounts and interpretations of the resurrection and the fact that they are mutually exclusive and set us on a collision course with our modern worldview and with every conceivable worldview, offending even those who seek wonders, love visions, and crave experience. Historical research reveals just how improbable, implausible, and historically impossible the event is. We would be more grateful if historical-critical research were more aware—and made us more aware—that even the most plausible reconstruction is only the most probable account of the improbable. It would be better if critical research did not make a last-minute treaty that overlooks these contradictions, enabling pastors to speak glibly about the resurrection as if they somehow knew what the word means. Here, the less we rely on historically plausible reconstructions, the better and more appropriate. Here, everything that is historically certain makes for uncertainty and leads away from revelation and faith, not toward them. Such an approach suggests that God's word fails at the very point where he intends to vouch for himself. Whoever thinks that he knows is precisely *the* person who does *not* know.[177] Whoever tries to explain the resurrection by appeal to analogies—whether from the history of religions, nature, the occult, or personal experience—only proves that he does not understand what Paul means by the resurrection. Paul is more liberal than the liberals and more trusting than the faithful. When he says "death," he means death. When he says "life," he means life. And in both cases, he means the whole—he means *God*. Everything that we consider to be "life" expires at death, and everything we consider to be "death" expires in the face of life. The step from one to the other, this unheard of step, which we could never take, *the* step that is the death of our life and the life of our death, is what Paul means by "resurrection." Clearly, he means a bodily resurrection because death is the death of the *body*, and the life that vanquishes death is also the life of the *body*. To speak of time is to speak of the body, and to speak of *eternity* in time is to speak about the resurrection of the body. Physical existence is material existence. Without material existence, there is no individual; without an individual, without a subject, there is no relation to God. Here, everything depends on interpreting the individual's relationship with God and God's relationship with the individual in *strictly* realistic terms. This applies equally to the reality of God's present moment in time.

Consequently, everything depends on recognizing the divergence between our interpretation of God's present moment and the reality itself. Everything depends on recognizing the final, comprehensive, radical answer and realizing that for *us* the answer is a question and no more. Paul regarded the resurrection as the point in history that assured his readers of *the extent* of the hope granted to them through

God's call and *the nature* of their Christian existence. Above all, it is for him the true meaning of the historic appearance of Jesus Christ; it is *the* absolute and unique meaning. For him, everything in Christ's appearance is understood on the basis of the crucifixion. Therefore he preaches Christ crucified and him alone; everything else that needs to be said about Christ can be summed up and included in this single event. If we ask what the crucifixion signifies, Paul would say (from God's point of view): resurrection, eternity, God's absolute present, the coexistence of the living and the dead, the eternal in the temporal, the imperishable with the perishable. And if we ask how we access this point, we are driven back to the unanswerable question, which could never be *our* question if it were not an answer in the form of a question, as is the case in Christ. It can be our question only as we perceive it in the light of Christ.

Second, Paul refers to *Christ's session at the right hand of God.* This is a second iteration of the resurrection event. It is the riddle of his rising from the dead, but viewed positively from God's realm. Christ is risen and now is seated at God's right hand. Is this "only a picture"? Certainly *not*! For Paul, God's right hand, meaning God's *power*, is as real and as vivid as anything he could envision. The movement from death to God's right hand occurs through the resurrection so that Christ now stands facing us as the transcendent and wholly other. The point that he occupies is transcendent, eternal, divine, and therefore ἐν τοῖς ἐπουρανίοις, in heaven. But this must be formulated precisely. There is a conception of the beyond or of heaven that is merely a superior version of life in this world. That is the only way that we can conceive of the heavenly realm apart from the reality of Christ. Absent Christ's reality, we can conceive of the heavenly only as the antithesis of human reality. By this account, he would be the elevated man. Our relationship with him would not be absolute. Our hope in him would not be total. The ground of our faith would not be unassailable. Therefore ὑπεράνω πάσης . . . means above everything that we can name, over every particular. The one who determines all things is not determined by them. The origin is not bound by cause and effect [*causa*]. His name is above all names [Phil. 2:9]. His rule is above every rule [v. 21]. Οὐ μόνον . . . , even the new aeon is a second-order reality; it transcends this world but is not ultimate reality. The point to which Paul witnesses stands beyond all transcendent realities. It is the absolutely transcendent. And for precisely this reason, it is God's immanence: πάντα ὑπέταξεν . . . In Christ, the world is a unity. Therein lies our hope. This unity overcomes the antitheses that presently determine our thinking and existence; it is the unity of heaven and earth. The point where Paul directs our attention is the *power* of God. It is the positive meaning of the resurrection: death is swallowed up in life just as life as we know it is swallowed up by death. But notice carefully: the world here is understood as a conquered realm. Divine sovereignty is predicated upon the resurrection. Unity depends on dissolution. The answer depends on the question. Paul reminds his readers that God *accomplishes* it all, and that in Christ *God* accomplishes it. *This* is the hope of their calling. To remember God's sovereignty is to remember the cross. The reality of God is the pathway—which is *no* pathway—to understanding what is disclosed here.

Third, Paul refers to Christ's enthronement: *God established Christ as the head of the church*. The extraordinary distinguishing mark of the Christian existence of believers is that the one who is risen and seated at God's right hand is *their* head. The "head over all" is *their* head. God in his majesty is *their* God. The eternal origin is *their* beginning. The mystery of the incarnation is *their* mystery. (1) They are his σῶμα, which means that in their diversity they are one in him. He is the divine meaning of their various individual identities, the unity in their diversity, the one unique individual who constitutes their individuality as Christians. (2) They are his πλήρωμα, the filling up of the empty form, which he signifies, in contrast to all that is human and the true fulfillment of all that is human. Their life is hidden with him in God (Col. 3:3). Paul reminds them of this hiddenness-with-Christ-in-God. *That* is the hope of their calling. Because they are in Christ, because they are the ἐκκλησία, called together by him, they are truly the object of God's blessing. Will they become what they truly are?[178]

A great divine *Forward!* into time, history, and humanity is announced and resounds here. That *Forward!* is Christ. But what does "Christ" mean? It means that God alone truly lives. Life as we know it is swallowed up by death (v. 20); it is one thing after another (vv.

20–21); it is our life in isolation (v. 23). Life itself must be found. And in Christ it *has* been found. But *finding* it in Christ is the issue for us. So let us be at peace with this *Forward!* which is no peace. To desire the unity of peace and unrest simply indicates that we do not understand either.[179]

# Ephesians 2–6

*Feb. 23, 1922*

My task today is to provide you with an outline of the contents of the last five chapters of Ephesians. This will take the form of a series of brief sketches. Obviously, this format does not permit me to provide the exegetical and systematic basis for my interpretation.

*2:1–10*. This section is clearly the counterpart of 1:20–23. There, Paul's concern is to supply his readers with the widest and most extensive survey of the blessings of God that they received in the gospel. There, the themes of the resurrection and the ascension of Christ effectively remind them that as believers they are engaged not with mere human matters but with God, not with time but with eternity. Here, it becomes clear that speaking about the mystery of Christ means speaking the mystery of human life. Like Christ, we too were *dead*. Our lives were a περιπατεῖν, following the course of this world and under the influence of the spirit of the world. Our φύσις was essentially disobedience and therefore the object of God's wrath (vv. 1–4). However, God has also made us *alive with* Christ, *together with* him. Ὄντας νεκροὺς συνεζωοποίησεν, συνήγειρεν, συνεκάθισεν (vv. 5 and 6). That is the paradox of our existence. This fundamental shift remains absolutely hidden from us. Its effects (v. 7) are in the future, temporally speaking; its origin and grounding (vv. 8–10) are in God. However, the relation of our life to this hidden renewal *really does exist*. In Christ, almighty God, the giver of life and source of all blessings, becomes the basis of our existence in the *past* as well as the *future*. In the power of his resurrection, Jesus is the midpoint,[180] which separates time, making the past truly the *past* and the future truly the *future*. The power of the resurrection is neither a contingent historical truth nor an eternal rational truth, to use Lessing's terminology.[181] Rather, it is God's truth in action and the expression of his will. It is not contingent. It is not a fact. It is not an idea. It is most emphatically *revelation*.

*2:11–22* introduces and develops an idea that is particularly close to the heart of the author of the epistle. In Christ, our existence here-and-now is so radically related to God's beyond,[182] and our entire known existence is brought so fully into the light of his eternal future, that the distinctions and antitheses that define our current existence are revealed to be conditional and provisional. What is the significance of the finite antithesis between the gentiles and Israel, between those who are far off and those who are near in light of the sublation[183] of the infinite antithesis between God and humanity, which is revealed in Christ as the hidden will of God? The *great* antithesis is the fundamental sublation of all *smaller* antitheses. The meaning and significance of this sublation is clear: there are people in the world without promise, without hope, and without God (vv. 11–12); but how could their plight be anything other than a parable, when the plight of such individuals is shared by *all* people and when the plight of *all* people is seen in Christ, in the light of the promise? The universal antitheses between the dead and the living, past and future, law and grace blunt the force of the antitheses between "them and us," gentile and Jew, Pharisees and worldlings, unbelievers and believers, outsiders and insiders. "For he is our peace, who has made us both one, and has broken down the dividing wall of hostility" (v. 14). Out of the two [gentile and Jew], he has created *one new* man in himself (v. 15). He has formed into one flesh those who were separated, reconciling them with God through the cross. He *himself* put to death the enmity (v. 16). He gives to those who were alienated from God access to the Father through *one* Spirit (v. 18). In him, aliens and strangers are fellow citizens and members of the household of God (v. 19). Christ constitutes the living relation of humanity to God, the cornerstone, the crisis as well as the ground of our existence. Consequently, the apparently absolute antitheses that divide us are revealed to be relative. Indeed, the distinctions become building blocks of a single house. Peace on earth is both a possibility and a mandate (vv. 20–21).

*3:1–13*. Here Paul explains that the idea, or rather his discovery, that gentiles and Jews are one in Christ is the distinctive feature of his own apostolic calling. He is emphatic that he has not been sent to preach to a general audience but is δέσμιος τοῦ Χριστοῦ "for you *gentiles*" (v. 1). As such, he is under obligation to deliver this specific message to the gentiles: "You, who were hopeless, now have hope; you, the godforsaken, belong to God; you, who were once far off, are now near." Paul's gospel, which he received by commission through revelation (vv. 2–3), is essentially the sublation of all relative, human antitheses in light of the absolute sublation, the οἰκονομία τῆς χάριτος τοῦ θεοῦ τῆς δοθείσης μοι. Paul regards this discovery as the defining feature of his age, the dawn of the Christian era, dividing the time before and *after* the historic appearance of Christ—not that the living relation between God and man is created or made possible for the first time (2:11–22 shows quite clearly that Paul took into account the saving presence of Christ even in the Old Testament). Rather, it is the dawn of a new age in the sense that gentiles are included as *co*heirs of this living relation, *co*partners of the promise in Christ Jesus through the gospel (v. 6). They have been *drawn into* that living relation that has always been granted to Israel. That is the mystery, which previous generations did not recognize but is now revealed (v. 5), the mystery of redemption, hidden from eternity in God, the creator of all things (v. 9). It has been vouchsafed to *him*, Paul himself, the least and the guiltiest among the saints,[184] to declare this mystery to the gentiles, his fellow trespassers. Consequently, his message and his life situation are inextricably bound (v. 8). This message must now be preached through the existence of the combined gentile and Jewish congregations of Christ on earth to the powers and authorities of the heavenly world, to all allegedly absolute authorities, which are in fact called into question by the reconciliation of *all* people and the consequent peace *among* all people (vv. 10–11). Christianity means the end of all "–isms," the complete reorganization and reorientation of our powers of perception, so that all mediated forms of God's presence are overshadowed by his unmediated presence, that is, the reality of God as he draws near to every person in Christ. This direct, unmediated divine access to every individual in Christ, this universalizing of the promise, this qualification of all historically given antitheses, is what is new and essential in the historic appearance of Jesus. The advent of his history signals the end of the history of religions. From now on, we can speak of "gentile" and "godforsaken" only in a qualified sense—in quotation marks, as it were—only in hope and love, without the tragic, harsh, and exclusive dimension that these appellations carry in the Old Testament. The wisdom of God in Christ and in his church is πολυποίκιλος. Because God's wisdom is manifold, polyvalent, and perdurable (v. 10), we can regard gentiles as future Christians and the godforsaken as anonymous children of God. Our righteousness cannot unite us to God, nor can our unrighteousness separate us from him. No, the righteousness of God both separates us from God and unites us to him, to use the conceptual framework of Romans. This is what Paul, messenger of salvation to the gentiles, reminds his readers.

*3:14–21* both concludes the preceding section and introduces what follows. It is the resumption of the apostle's prayer for his readers that commenced in 1:15–19. Paul bows before the Father, who epitomizes the fatherhood in all relationships in heaven and on earth and who is the reality of God's "beyond" in every contingent relation of cause and effect, of creator and created in this world. These relations can exist because of him. They are merely parables and images of him. *He* must give what his readers need to strengthen the inner person and so that Christ may dwell in their hearts through faith; so that they may be so grounded in love; so that nothing may disturb the community's life in Christ; so that any claims about what is "mine" and what is "yours" may disappear (vv. 15–17); so that they realize that the truth is always multifaceted and that the love of Christ surpasses all human knowledge, be it individual, direct, discursive, animate, or inanimate (vv. 18–19); so that we may know that God delights to give more than we can desire or imagine. The ἐκκλησία, Christ Jesus himself, enfleshed in their midst and called together by him (vv. 20–21), is the domain where God gives this insight and where it is understood—where God appears, saying "I am!" and where we take the *risk* of understanding the sinful, lost world exclusively through its connection with God. Here, at the conclusion of chapter 3, we reach the summit of the entire letter.

In *4:1–16* the prayer becomes an *admonition* to preserve the peace that is given to humanity in Christ, to regard the relative human antitheses and unvarnished human existence in the reconciling light of the absolute antithesis between God and humanity. "Be diligent to preserve the unity of the Spirit in the bond of peace" (v. 3). We must hear this admonition in context. Paul urges peace not for the sake of peace but for the sake of God's honor and as the consequence of their *calling* as Christians. Their calling is a call to *one* hope. *That* is the bond of peace. The εἷς, μία, ἕν, and so on in verses 4–6 should not be emphasized at the expense of the nouns they modify; they are equally important. We are one *body* and one *Spirit*. We are called to one *hope*, one *Lord*, one *faith*, one *baptism*, one *God* and *Father*. In Christ, we encounter the incomparable new *reality of God*—that is the foundation of Paul's admonition. The reality of God, which humbles and exalts us, which abases us so profoundly and restores us so powerfully, *is* the peace, *is* the one undeniable reality, despite our relative human antitheses. If we did not believe in one *God*, it would be pointless for us to believe in *one* God. Indifference is a poor foundation for tolerance. But unity in *God* constitutes the freedom of the *individual*, just as he is. Unity is the consequence of belonging to God. Life in Christ is the journey from life enclosed by death to life; it comprehends all existence, from the most vexing distinctions imaginable to the smaller antitheses that divide us (vv. 7–10). (You will find the same basis for freedom and unity in Rom. 14:7–11.) The distinctive personality and situation of each individual is merely *preparation* for the service and upbuilding of the body of Christ (v. 12). The distinctiveness of each person must be "given" by Christ (v. 11). The service itself must be done within the limits of our individuality. This limit is bracketed [sublated] by the perfect humanity of Christ, revealing the eternal dimension of the divinely given uniqueness (v. 13). But there is a difference between the now and the not yet. From our present status "here and now" we can only anticipate the "not yet." We do so by avoiding all sectarianism (v. 14), honoring the truth in love (v. 15), and maturing in Christ until we come to the unity of the faith in the knowledge of the Son of God (v. 13)—which is not simply the goal of growth in Christ but the fulfillment of that goal that surpasses all human growth. This goal, which lies beyond life as we know it, determines and characterizes our earthly journey. Thus our hope becomes our peace. Peace is upon the mountain.[185] We have not yet reached the mountain. But we can lift our eyes to the hills, from whence cometh our help.[186]

*4:17–24* applies the admonition to the overall realm of ethics. Paul does not preach morals; he witnesses (v. 17) to the consequence of the great antithesis that illuminates the Christian life, the crisis between this world and the next that is revealed in Christ and has overtaken believers. God's revelation is an attack upon the human creature. Real Christianity is dangerous. But Christians have already succumbed to this danger. They have developed a God-given sense of hearing for Christ's voice; they know how things stand in relation to Jesus (v. 21). According to Paul, here as in Romans 6:1–14, overcoming evil is not a matter of obligation but a matter of course. Retreat is not an option. The decisive step has already been taken. The new light already envelops them. They have God's promise. How could anyone who has God's promise want to live in the past? To have God's promise is to lay aside the old and to put on the new (vv. 22–23). So the admonition is analytic, not synthetic. It means: become what you are! and not what you are not! But to become what we already are is a continual task for anyone, something we must *call to mind* again and again as long as we live. Therefore admonition is necessary: be renewed by the Spirit in your *thinking* (v. 23). *Repent!* so that God's reality *may become* the life-transforming reality of your life. We must continually receive the knowledge of God so that we understand that as sinners we are no different from other people, and we must continuously receive to understand that we cannot remain sinners and live as others live. The *vita christiana*[187] is and will always be a dynamic movement forward, never arrival.

*4:25–5:20* explores the positive and negative consequences of the great shadow that God casts upon our lives, the difficult attack and the ongoing battle in which we find ourselves from all quarters. It is impossible to give even a schematic account of the passage. I can only offer a paraphrase of its basic direction. A relationship with God makes a person attentive and vigilant. He knows that he has been given a sacred and indestructible trust. He regards the kingdom of God as the one thing needful. Step by step he receives new clarity and new freedoms that allow him to renounce the old ways, even though he knows that his own efforts will always be mere piecework, merely provisional, rudimentary, and accompanied by constant struggle. The fact that life has become difficult is a sign or indication for him of the mercy of God vouchsafed to him. The weight of the divine imperative oppresses only those who stand in grace. The knowledge of God comes with fear and trembling [Job 4:14; Ps. 55:5; Phil. 2:12]—we cannot avoid it. But we are ready for it. Under the influence of Spirit, we are open to correction. We can be directed. The Spirit of freedom gives us freedom to change. This is the new element in the Christian ethos. In such an ethos, the prevailing question is: Do we have ears to hear [cf. Matt. 11:15; Mark 4:9, etc.], and do we believe in the light so that we may become children of light [John 12:36; cf. Eph. 5:9]? If this question is not constantly before us, Christian zeal in any form or fashion will be of little avail. However, if this question weighs on us and disquiets us, if it is the basis of our Christian ethos, then Paul's admonitions will be written in our hearts and relevant in every situation.

*5:21–6:9*. This passage stands out in the overall scheme of the admonition. It concerns relationships between husbands and wives, parents and children, masters and slaves. Luther considered it "a rule for the Christian household." But it should be noted that neither Paul nor the rest of the New Testament attaches any particular importance to human forms of community per se; therefore, the passage should not be read as a rudimentary form of social ethics. What matters to Paul is not the establishment, maintenance, and welfare of the family as such but that every aspect of a person's life be seen in the light of the great antithesis, including this most significant and concrete reality of life. Even in their natural state, these relationships of ordered interdependence reflect our fundamental dependence on God in Christ; they are honored as Christian relationships to the extent that they reflect the divine-human relation. The obedience enjoined here is appropriate for that purpose and that purpose alone. The fear of Christ (5:21) both justifies these relationships and guarantees that they are not absolute relationships. Marriage is a mystery (5:32): it is by nature finite, yet it points to the promise of a future eternal transformation. Likewise, the relationships of parents to children exist for the purpose of training and admonition unto the Lord (6:4). The social orders witness to *one* Lord who orders all things, namely, God. This passage is not as conservative or implausible as it sounds when read out of context. It is more revolutionary than it may first appear, but the revolution to which it witnesses is from above. The very fact that it is radical explains its conservative tenor. The restoration of the human orders of creation occurs through an indirect attack upon these relationships in their current state—not externally but internally and from the roots. It attacks them by allowing them to remain!

The conclusion of the letter, *6:10–24*, makes us acutely aware that, humanly speaking, Christians are called to prepare, to contend, and to struggle each new moment as earnestly as if it were the first, the beginning of the journey. True theology is and will always be *theologia viatorum*.[188] But if all we *can* be is pilgrims, then pilgrims we should *be*. We are to be clothed with the πανοπλία, the armor of Christ, as we learn from the familiar illustration here (6:10–17). As God's combatants, Christians are to take their stand like Jacob, in the dark of night until the dawn of the new day, saying: "I will not let you go unless you bless me!" [Gen. 32:26]. "Watch and pray!" [cf. 6:18] is Paul's motto—for his readers and for himself.[189] Paul commends himself to their prayers; and his own extremity is what enables him to comfort others. The ambiguity of our existence corresponds to the liveliness of our hope; and hope in turn enables us to live to the glory of God, neither blind to life's difficulties nor resigned to them. The essence of grace is to love the Lord Jesus Christ ἐν ἀφθαρσίᾳ (v. 24), confident that he who conducts God's affairs in heaven will also tend to ours. That, in conclusion, is what Paul hopes for himself and for his readers.

# For Further Reading

## Related Works by Karl Barth


Barth, Karl. *The Epistle to the Philippians: 40th Anniversary Edition*. Translated by James W. Leitch. Louisville: Westminster John Knox, 2002.

———. *The Epistle to the Romans*. Translated by Edwyn C. Hoskyns. London: Oxford University Press, 1968.

———. *The Göttingen Dogmatics: Instruction in the Christian Religion*. Vol. 1. Edited by Hannelotte Reiffen. Translated by Geoffrey W. Bromiley. Grand Rapids: Eerdmans, 1991.

———. *The Theology of John Calvin*. Translated by Geoffrey W. Bromiley. Grand Rapids: Eerdmans, 1995.

———. *The Theology of the Reformed Confessions, 1923*. Translated and edited by Darrell L. Guder and Judith J. Guder. Columbia Series in Reformed Theology. Louisville: Westminster John Knox, 2002.

———. *The Theology of Schleiermacher: Lectures at Göttingen, Winter Semester of 1923/24*. Edited by Dietrich Ritschl. Translated by Geoffrey W. Bromiley. With "Concluding Unscientific Postscript," translated by George Hunsinger. Grand Rapids: Eerdmans, 1982.

———. *The Word of God and the Word of Man*. Translated by Douglas Horton. London: Hodder & Stoughton, 1928.

Barth, Karl, and Eduard Thurneysen. *Revolutionary Theology in the Making: Barth-Thurneysen Correspondence, 1914–1925*. Translated by James D. Smart. Richmond: John Knox, 1964.

**Other Works**

Asprey, Christopher. *Eschatological Presence in Karl Barth's Göttingen Theology*. Oxford: Oxford University Press, 2010.

Barth, Markus. *Ephesians: Introduction Translation, and Commentary*. 2 vols. Anchor Bible 34–34A. Garden City, NY: Doubleday, 1974.

Bender, Kimlyn J. "Scripture and Canon in Karl Barth's Early Theology." In *Confessing Christ for Church and World: Studies in Modern Theology*, 145–77. Downers Grove, IL: IVP Academic, 2014.

Burnett, Richard E. *Karl Barth's Theological Exegesis: The Hermeneutical Principles of the* Römerbrief *Period*. Grand Rapids: Eerdmans, 2004.

Busch, Eberhard. *Karl Barth: His Life from Letters and Autobiographical Texts*. Translated by John Bowden. Philadelphia: Fortress, 1976.

Ford, David F. "Barth's Interpretation of the Bible." In *Karl Barth: Studies of His Theological Method*, edited by Stephen W. Sykes, 55–87. Oxford: Clarendon, 1979.

Hunsinger, George. "Beyond Literalism and Expressivism: Karl Barth's Hermeneutical Realism." *Modern Theology* 3 (1987): 209–23.

———, ed. *Thy Word Is Truth: Barth on Scripture*. Grand Rapids: Eerdmans, 2012.

Jüngel, Eberhard. *Karl Barth: A Theological Legacy*. Translated by Garrett E. Paul. Philadelphia: Westminster, 1986.

McCormack, Bruce L. "Historical-Criticism and Dogmatic Interest in Karl Barth's Theological Exegesis of the New Testament." In *Biblical Hermeneutics in Historical Perspective: Studies in Honor of Karlfried Froelich on His Sixtieth Birthday*, edited by Mark S. Burrows and Paul Rorem, 322–38. Grand Rapids: Eerdmans, 1991.

———. *Karl Barth's Critically Realistic Dialectical Theology: Its Genesis and Development, 1909–1936*. Oxford: Clarendon, 1995.

Oakes, Kenneth. *Reading Karl Barth: A Companion to Karl Barth's "Epistle to the Romans."* Eugene, OR: Cascade, 2011.

Watson, Francis. "The Bible." In *The Cambridge Companion to Karl Barth*, edited by John Webster, 57–71. Cambridge Companions to Religion. Cambridge: Cambridge University Press, 2000.

Webster, John. *Barth's Earlier Theology: Four Studies*. London: T&T Clark, 2005.

Westerholm, Martin. *The Ordering of the Christian Mind: Karl Barth and Theological Rationality*. Oxford: Oxford University Press, 2015.

Wood, Donald. *Barth's Theology of Interpretation*. Barth Studies. Aldershot: Ashgate, 2007.

# Notes

**Editor's Introduction**

1. See Eberhard Busch's overview of this period in *Karl Barth: His Life from Letters and Autobiographical Texts*, trans. John Bowden (Philadelphia: Fortress, 1976), 60–153. For a substantive treatment of the significance of the "early Barth" for the development of the entire course of his thought, see the classic study by Bruce L. McCormack, *Karl Barth's Critically Realistic Dialectical Theology: Its Genesis and Development 1909–1936* (Oxford: Clarendon, 1995), especially 207–323. Christopher Asprey surveys the cross-currency between themes of eschatology and revelation in Barth's texts from the early period in *Eschatological Presence in Karl Barth's Göttingen Theology* (Oxford: Oxford University Press, 2010). To date, the most fulsome treatment of Barth's exegesis during the early 1920s is Richard E. Burnett, *Karl Barth's Theological Exegesis: The Hermeneutical Principles of the* Römerbrief *Period* (Grand Rapids: Eerdmans, 2004).

2. The standard German texts of the two editions of *Der Römerbrief* are found in the *Gesamtausgabe* (abbreviated below as GA following the first full citation): Karl Barth, *Der Römerbrief*, Erste Fassung, 1919, hg. Hermann Schmidt, *Karl Barth Gesamtausgabe* 16 (Zürich: TVZ, 1985); idem, *Der Römerbrief*, Zweite Fassung, 1922, hg. Cornelis van der Kooi und Katja Tolstaja, GA 47 (Zürich: TVZ, 2010). The 1922 edition is available in English as Karl Barth, *The Epistle to the Romans*, trans. Edwyn C. Hoskyns (London: Oxford University Press, 1968). The 1919 edition of *Der Römerbrief* remains untranslated. On *The Epistle to the Romans*, see the helpful supplementary text by Kenneth Oakes, *Reading Karl Barth: A Companion to Karl Barth's "Epistle to the Romans"* (Eugene, OR: Cascade, 2011), which also contains a summary of the development of the two German editions.

3. See the editor's "Vorwort" in Karl Barth, *Erklärungen des Epheser- und des Jakobusbriefes, 1919–1929*, hg. Jörg-Michael Bohnet, GA 46 (Zürich: TVZ, 2009), vii.

4. These early lecture cycles are available in critical editions in the *Gesamtausgabe* and also, with the exception of the Zwingli lectures, in English: Karl Barth, *Die Theologie Calvins, 1922*, hg. Hans Scholl, GA 23 (Zürich: TVZ, 1993); → ET, idem, *The Theology of John Calvin*, trans. Geoffrey W. Bromiley (Grand Rapids: Eerdmans, 1995); idem, *Die Theologie Zwinglis, Vorlesung Göttingen 1922/23*, hg. Matthias Freudenberg, GA 40 (Zürich: TVZ, 2004); → no ET; idem, *Die Theologie der reformierten Bekenntnisschriften, 1923*, hg. Eberhard Busch, GA 30 (Zürich: TVZ, 1998); → ET, idem, *The Theology of the Reformed Confessions, 1923*, trans. and ed. Darrell L. Guder and Judith J. Guder, Columbia Series in Reformed Theology (Louisville: Westminster John Knox, 2002); idem, *Die Theologie Schleiermachers, Vorlesung Göttingen 1923/24*, hg. Dietrich Ritschl, GA 11 (Zürich: TVZ, 1978); → ET, idem, *The Theology of Schleiermacher: Lectures at Göttingen, Winter Semester of 1923/24*, ed. Dietrich Ritschl, trans. Geoffrey W. Bromiley, with "Concluding Unscientific Postscript," trans. George Hunsinger (Grand Rapids: Eerdmans, 1982).

5. In the Gesamtausgabe: Karl Barth, «Unterricht in der christlichen Religion», Teil 1: Prolegomena, 1924, hg. Hannelotte Reiffen, GA 17 (Zürich: TVZ, 1985); idem, «Unterricht in der christlichen Religion», Teil 2: Die Lehre von Gott/Die Lehre vom Menschen, 1924/25, hg. Hinrich Stoevesandt, GA 20 (Zürich: TVZ, 1990); idem, «Unterricht in der christlichen Religion», Teil 3: Die Lehre von der Versöhnung/Erlösung, 1925/26, hg. Hinrich Stoevesandt, GA 38 (Zürich: TVZ, 2003). The first volume of the English translation is available as Karl Barth, *The Göttingen Dogmatics: Instruction in the Christian Religion*, vol. 1, ed. Hannelotte Reiffen, trans. Geoffrey W. Bromiley (Grand Rapids: Eerdmans, 1991).

6. The exegetical lectures from the Göttingen period are gradually being received into the *Gesamtausgabe*. The lectures on James from the Winter Semester of 1922/23, which Barth titled *Erklärung des Jakobusbriefes*, are found in GA 46, 157–529. They are published in parallel (on verso) with the lectures on the epistle Barth delivered in Münster in the *Wintersemester* 1928/29. Barth himself released for publication the lectures on 1 Corinthians 15 and Philippians, and these are available as Karl Barth, *Die Auferstehung der Toten: Eine akademische Vorlesung über 1.Kor.15* (München: Kaiser, 1924); → ET, idem, *The Resurrection of the Dead*, trans. H. J. Stenning (New York: Revell, 1933); idem, *Erklärung des Philipperbriefes* (München: Kaiser, 1928); → ET, idem, *The Epistle to the Philippians: 40th Anniversary Edition*, trans. James W. Leitch [from the German 6th ed., 1947] (Louisville: Westminster John Knox, 2002). The lectures on 1 John, Colossians, and the Sermon on the Mount to date remain unpublished.

7. A critical German edition of the 1921/22 lectures on the Heidelberg Catechism is currently in process. They have yet to appear in English.

8. Christopher Asprey, "Remarks concerning Barth's Ephesians lectures in Göttingen (1921/22) on the Occasion of Their Posthumous Publication," in

*Letter from the Karl Barth-Archives* 11 (December 10, 2009), 1 (https://karlbarth.unibas.ch/fileadmin/downloads/letter11/Letter11-Asprey.pdf).

9. GA 46.

**Translating Barth's Ephesians Lectures**

1. Present volume, 76, 78, 75.

2. Karl Barth, *The Theology of John Calvin*, trans. Geoffrey W. Bromiley (Grand Rapids: Eerdmans, 1995), 389.

3. Perhaps we should not press the distinction too far, and in any event, it is hard to find exact English equivalents to help us do so. Barth's exegetical lectures, like Luther's and Calvin's expository lectures on the Bible, are neither sermons nor academic commentaries but combinations of both elements.

4. Rudolf Bultmann, "Karl Barth, *The Resurrection of the Dead*," in *Faith and Understanding*, ed. Robert F. Funk, trans. Louise Pettibone Smith (Philadelphia: Fortress, 1989), 66–94. The phrase mentioned here is on page 86.

5. I was alerted to the significance of intertextual associations in theological exegesis by R. R. Reno's address "Biblical Theology and Theological Exegesis" at the Conference on Biblical Hermeneutics, University of St Andrews, 2002; cf. John J. O'Keefe and R. R. Reno, *Sanctified Vision: An Introduction to Early Christian Interpretation of the Bible* (Baltimore: Johns Hopkins University Press, 2005).

6. Present volume, 61.

7. Present volume, 136.

8. Hans-Anton Drewes proposed this metaphor during a conversation at the Karl Barth-Archiv, Basel, August 8, 2004.

9. Present volume, 81.

10. Present volume, 81.

11. John Webster, "Barth's Lectures on the Gospel of John," in *Thy Word Is Truth: Barth on Scripture*, ed. George Hunsinger (Grand Rapids: Eerdmans, 2012), 21.

12. The critical edition of the German text is found in Karl Barth, *Erklärungen des Epheser- und des Jakobusbriefes, 1919–1929*, hg. Jörg-Michael Bohnet, *Karl Barth Gesamtausgabe* 46 (Zürich: TVZ, 2009).

13. This is the approach adopted by Darrell L. Guder and Judith J. Guder. See "Translator's Preface," in Karl Barth, *The Theology of the Reformed Confessions, 1923*, trans. and ed. Darrell L. Guder and Judith J. Guder, Columbia Series in Reformed Theology (Louisville: Westminster John Knox, 2002), xi–xiii.

14. This strategy is an improvement over older translations of Barth's exegetical lectures, such as Stenning's rendering of the series on 1 Corinthains, which omits the Greek text. See Karl Barth, *The Resurrection of the Dead*, trans. H. J. Stenning (New York: Revell, 1933).

15. Vladimir Nabokov, "The Art of Translation," *New Republic*, August 4, 1941, 160–62; quotes from 160.

**Barth, Ephesians, and the Practice of Theological Exegesis**

1. Karl Barth, *Erklärungen des Epheser- und des Jakobusbriefes, 1919–1929*, hg. Jörg-Michael Bohnet, *Karl Barth Gesamtausgabe* 46 [hereafter GA 46] (Zürich: TVZ, 2009), 91n; → ET, below, Karl Barth, "Exposition of Ephesians, Winter Semester 1921–22" [hereafter *Ephesians*]. For the biographical context, see Eberhard Busch, *Karl Barth: His Life from Letters and Autobiographical Texts*, trans. John Bowden (Philadelphia: Fortress, 1976), 126–34.

2. GA 46, ix.

3. Karl Barth, *Der Römerbrief*, Zweite Fassung, 1922, hg. Cornelis van der Kooi und Katja Tolstaja, *Karl Barth Gesamtausgabe* 47 [hereafter GA 47] (Zürich: TVZ, 2010), 3–4; → ET, idem, *The Epistle to the Romans* [hereafter *Romans*], trans. Edwyn C. Hoskyns (London: Oxford University Press, 1968), 1–2.

4. GA 47, 11–16; *Romans*, 6–10.

5. GA 46, 45–50; present volume, 55.

6. GA 46, 45; present volume, 55.

7. GA 46, 46–47; present volume, 56–58.

8. GA 46, 46–50; present volume, 58.

9. GA 46, 63–67; present volume, 65–71.

10. Tertullian, *Adversus Marcionem* 5.17.1.

11. Fritz Barth, *Einleitung in das Neue Testament* (Gütersloh: Bertelsmann, 1908), 70–77.

12. GA 46, 46; present volume, 56, 71.

13. F. Barth, *Einleitung*, 71 (my translation, as in the quotations that follow).

14. GA 46, 49; present volume, 58.

15. F. Barth, *Einleitung*, 71. K. Barth, GA 46, 65; present volume, 72. At one point there is verbal overlap. Fritz Barth: "Nun ist es schwer denkbar, dass *der Name der angesehenen* Gemeinde *von Ephesus* aus dem Briefeingang sollte getilgt worden sein" (*Einleitung*, 71). Karl Barth: Ephesians was a circular letter that "die Kirche mit *dem angesehen Namen von Ephesus* ergänzte" (GA 46, 65; italics added in both cases).

16. F. Barth, *Einleitung*, iv.

17. GA 46, 50. The Bengel reference has not been traced. Cf. present volume, 59.

18. GA 46, 45; present volume, 55.

19. GA 46, 67; present volume, 72.

20. GA 46, 133; present volume, 112.

21. GA 46, 70–73; present volume, 74–76. Cf. GA 47, 207–8; *Romans*, 150–52.

22. GA 46, 70; present volume, 75. Cf. GA 47, 207; *Romans*, 151.

23. GA 46, 72; present volume, 76. Cf. GA 47, 207; *Romans*, 151.

24. GA 46, 72; present volume, 76. Cf. GA 47, 208; *Romans*, 151. Modifications (italicized) to these sentences from the Romans commentary are purely stylistic: "Nicht im Geringsten hört der Mensch etwa auf, ein Wartender, nur ein Wartender zu sein, ein Hoffender, der nicht schaut. *Er wartet und hofft aber* auf Gott, und das eben ist sein Friede mit *ihm*."

25. GA 46, 106; present volume, 117.

26. GA 47, 207, 208; *Romans*, 151–52.

27. GA 47, 13; *Romans*, 7.

28. GA 47, 14; *Romans*, 8.

29. "Wir denken an Johannes den Täufer auf Grünewalds Kreuzigungsbild mit seiner in fast unmöglicher Weise zeigenden Hand. Diese Hand ist's, die in der Bibel dokumentiert ist" (Karl Barth, "Biblische Fragen, Einsichten und Ausblicke" [1920], repr. in Jürgen Moltmann, hg., *Anfänge der dialektischen Theologie*, Theologische Bücherei 17 [Gütersloh: Kaiser, 1962], 1:58; → ET, idem, *The Word of God and the Word of Man*, trans. Douglas Horton [London: Hodder & Stoughton, 1928], 65).

30. A reference to *God's* love would require a significant departure from the Greek word order, as in William Tyndale's translation: "acordynge as he had chosen us in hym *throwe love* before the foundation of the worlde was layde that we shulde be saynts and without blame in his sight."

31. Augustine, *De doctrina christiana* 3.2.2–3.7 (on correct punctuation and pronunciation).

32. GA 46, 54; present volume, 70.

33. *Codex Sinaiticus: Facsimile Edition* (London: British Library, 2010), Q-84-f.4v. Available online at http://codexsinaiticus.org/en/.

34. GA 46, xxix, 63n, 121; cf. present volume, 116.

35. Eberhard Nestle, *Novum Testamentum Graece cum apparatu critico ex editionibus et libris manu scriptis collecto* (Stuttgart: Privilegierte Württembergische Bibelanstalt, 1898, 1899, 1901).

36. GA 46, 102; present volume, 79.

37. GA 46, 102; present volume, 40.

38. GA 46, 102; present volume, 74.

39. GA 46, 79; present volume, 82.

40. Martin Dibelius, *Die Briefe des Apostels Paulus. II. Die neun kleinen Briefe*, Handbuch zum Neuen Testament (Göttingen: Vandenhoeck & Ruprecht, 1913), 46*. Cf. Barth, GA 46, 79; present volume, 81–82. Barth already refers to Dibelius's analysis in exegetical notes on the Letter to the Ephesians dating from 1919–20 (GA 46, 3; present volume, 56, 71, 81–82).

41. GA 46, 79; present volume, 81.

42. GA 46, 45, 67; present volume, 72. Cf. Dibelius, *Die Briefe des Apostels Paulus*, 47*, 66*.

43. GA 46, 47; present volume, 56. Cf. Dibelius, *Die Briefe des Apostels Paulus*, 113–14.

44. GA 46, 66; present volume, 71. Cf. Dibelius, *Die Briefe des Apostels Paulus*, 96.

45. The term is still fundamental to Schleiermacher's hermeneutics, where "grammatical" interpretation investigates a text's use of language while "psychological" interpretation views it in relation to its author. See Friedrich Schleiermacher, *Hermeneutik und Kritik: Mit einem Anhang sprachphilosophischer*

*Texte Schleiermachers*, ed. Manfred Frank, Suhrkamp Taschenbuch Wissenschaft 211 (Frankfurt am Main: Suhrkamp, 1977), 79 [§§6, 7]). During the nineteenth century, "grammatical" seems to have been displaced by "historical-critical."

46. See Francis Watson, "Does Historical Criticism Exist?," in *Theological Theology: Essays in Honour of John Webster*, ed. R. David Nelson, Darren Sarisky, and Justin Stratis, T&T Clark Theology (London: Bloomsbury T&T Clark, 2015), 307–18.

47. GA 46, 79–80; present volume, 82.

48. GA 46, 67–68; present volume, 55.

49. GA 46, 135–37; present volume, 127–30.

50. GA 46, 136; present volume, 129.

51. Konrad Hammann, *Rudolf Bultmann: Eine Biographie* (Tübingen: Mohr Siebeck, 2009), 134–47.

52. GA 46, 138–39; present volume, 131.

53. GA 46, 139–40; present volume, 131–32.

54. Adolf von Harnack, *Das Wesen des Christentums: Sechzehn Vorlesungen vor Studierenden aller Fakultäten im Wintersemester 1899/1900 an der Universität Berlin gehalten* (Leipzig: J. C. Hinrichs, 1900); → ET, idem, *What Is Christianity? Lectures Delivered in the University of Berlin during the Winter-Term 1899–1900* (London: Williams & Norgate; New York: G. P. Putnam's Sons, 1904).

55. GA 46, 141; present volume, 132–33.

56. GA 46, 144; present volume, 134–36.

57. GA 46, 142; present volume, 132–35.

58. GA 46, 143–44; present volume, 134.

59. Hammann, *Rudolf Bultmann*, 102.

60. Ibid., 136; Cf. Busch, *Karl Barth*, 135–36.

61. Originally published in four consecutive issues of the *Christliche Welt* (36.18–21 [1922]); repr. in Moltmann, *Anfänge der dialektischen Theologie*, 1:119–42; ET in *The Beginnings of Dialectic Theology*, ed. James M. Robinson (Richmond: John Knox, 1968), 100–120.

62. In §19.2 of the *Kirchliche Dogmatik*, Barth underlines the close relationship between the content and form of Holy Scripture in its witness to divine revelation and criticizes the assumption of modern historicism that we should penetrate behind the texts to the early history of Israel or to the life of the historical Jesus. There is, he argues, an essential connection between his own recovery of Scripture's relation to its content (its *Gegenständlichkeit*) and the recovery of its corresponding form (*die jener Gegenständlichkeit entsprechende Gestalt*) in the form-critical work of Dibelius, Bultmann, and Schmidt. See Karl Barth, *Kirchliche Dogmatik* I.2, *Studienausgabe*, vol. 5, *Die Heilige Schrift* (Zürich: TVZ, 1993), 547; → ET, idem, *Church Dogmatics* I.2, *The Doctrine of the Word of God*, trans. Geoffrey W. Bromiley, G. T. Thomson, and Harold Knight (London: T&T Clark Continuum, 2010), 494.

63. Rudolf Bultmann, *Die Geschichte der synoptischen Tradition*, Forschungen zur Religion und Literatur des Alten und Neuen Testaments 29 (Göttingen:

Vandenhoeck & Ruprecht, 1921), 308–16*; → ET, idem, *The History of the Synoptic Tradition*, 2nd ed., trans. John Marsh (Oxford: Blackwell, 1963), 284–91.

**"A Relation beyond All Relations": God and Creatures in Barth's Lectures on Ephesians, 1921–22**

1. See Karl Barth, *The Theology of John Calvin*, trans. Geoffrey W. Bromiley (Grand Rapids: Eerdmans, 1995); idem, *Die Theologie Zwinglis, Vorlesung Göttingen 1922/23*, hg. Matthias Freudenberg, *Karl Barth Gesamtausgabe* [hereafter GA] 40 (Zürich: TVZ, 2004); idem, *The Theology of the Reformed Confessions, 1923*, trans. and ed. Darrell L. Guder and Judith J. Guder (Louisville: Westminster John Knox, 2002); idem, *The Theology of Schleiermacher: Lectures at Göttingen, Winter Semester of 1923/24*, ed. Dietrich Ritschl, trans. Geoffrey W. Bromiley, with "Concluding Unscientific Postscript," trans. George Hunsinger (Grand Rapids: Eerdmans, 1982).

2. Karl Barth, *«Unterricht in der christlichen Religion», Teil 1: Prolegomena, 1924*, hg. Hannelotte Reiffen, GA 17 (Zürich: TVZ, 1985); idem, *«Unterricht in der christlichen Religion», Teil 2: Die Lehre von Gott/Die Lehre vom Menschen, 1924/25*, hg. Hinrich Stoevesandt, GA 20 (Zürich: TVZ, 1990); idem, *«Unterricht in der christlichen Religion», Teil 3: Die Lehre von der Versöhnung/Erlösung, 1925/26*, hg. Hinrich Stoevesandt, GA 38 (Zürich: TVZ, 2003). The final lectures in the series, on eschatology, were delivered in Münster. The first volume of the Gesamtausgabe series is available in English as Karl Barth, *The Göttingen Dogmatics: Instruction in the Christian Religion*, vol. 1, ed. Hannelotte Reiffen, trans. Geoffrey W. Bromiley (Grand Rapids: Eerdmans, 1991).

3. Karl Barth, *Die Auferstehung der Toten: Eine akademische Vorlesung über 1.Kor.15* (München: Kaiser, 1924); → ET, idem, *The Resurrection of the Dead*, trans. H. J. Stenning (New York: Revell, 1933). The English translation is inaccurate and incomplete.

4. Karl Barth, *Erklärung des Philipperbriefes* (München: Kaiser, 1928); → ET, idem, *Epistle to the Philippians: 40th Anniversary Edition*, trans. James W. Leitch [from the German 6th ed., 1947] (Louisville: Westminster John Knox, 2002).

5. Karl Barth, *Erklärungen des Epheser- und des Jakobusbriefes, 1919–1929*, hg. Jörg-Michael Bohnet, GA 46 (Zürich: TVZ, 2009).

6. See Nina-Dorothee Mützlitz, *Gottes Wort als Wirklichkeit. Die Paulus-Rezeption des jungen Karl Barth (1906–1927)*, Neukirchener Theologie (Neukirchen-Vluyn: Neukirchener Verlag, 2013); Martin Westerholm, *The Ordering of the Christian Mind. Karl Barth and Theological Rationality* (Oxford: Oxford University Press, 2015).

7. Barth, *Theology of John Calvin*, 388–89.

8. Ibid., 389 (emphasis original).

9. *Karl Barth – Eduard Thurneysen Briefwechsel I. 1913–1921*, hg. Eduard Thurneysen, GA 3 (Zürich: TVZ, 1973), 268–69.

10. Karl Barth, *Predigten, 1919*, hg. Hermann Schmidt, GA 39 (Zürich: TVZ, 2003), 173–334.

11. This material is available in GA 46, 3–44.

12. Present volume, 126 (emphasis original).

13. Barth, *Theology of the Reformed Confessions*, 38–64; see also idem, "Das Schriftprinzip der reformierten Kirche," in *Vorträge und kleinere Arbeiten, 1922–1925*, hg. Holger Finze, GA 19 (Zürich: TVZ, 1990), 500–544.

14. In this connection, Barth's remarks on "history as life's teacher" in his opening lecture on Calvin in the 1922 series are illuminating (see Barth, *Theology of John Calvin*, 1–9). See, further, Hinrich Stoevesandt, "Barths Calvinvorlesung als Station seiner theologischen Biographie," in *Karl Barth und Johannes Calvin: Karl Barths Göttinger Calvin-Vorlesung von 1922*, hg. Hans Scholl (Neukirchen-Vluyn: Neukirchener Verlag, 1995), 107–24.

15. Present volume, 72.

16. Present volume, 132–33 (emphasis original).

17. Present volume, 133 (emphasis original).

18. Present volume, 134.

19. Present volume, 134.

20. Present volume, 58–59.

21. See here the 1917 lecture "The New World in the Bible," in Karl Barth, *The Word of God and Theology*, trans. Amy Marga (London: T&T Clark, 2011), 15–29.

22. Present volume, 59–60 (emphasis original).

23. A little later, however, Barth notes briefly that apostles are "envoys who are instructed and equipped with power" (present volume, 61).

24. Present volume, 61.

25. Present volume, 61.

26. Present volume, 62–63.

27. Present volume, 64.

28. Present volume, 76–77 (emphasis original).

29. Present volume, 77 (emphasis original).

30. Present volume, 97.

31. Present volume, 80–81.

32. Present volume, 111.

33. Present volume, 111 (emphasis original).

34. Present volume, 112 (emphasis original).

35. Present volume, 112 (emphasis original).

36. Present volume, 89.

37. Present volume, 89.

38. Present volume, 97.

39. Present volume, 102 (emphasis original).

40. Present volume, 89 (emphasis original).

41. Present volume, 123.

42. Christopher Asprey, *Eschatological Presence in Karl Barth's Göttingen Theology* (Oxford: Oxford University Press, 2010), 24 (emphasis original).

43. Present volume, 60.
44. Present volume, 61.
45. Present volume, 61.
46. Present volume, 82–83.
47. Present volume, 123–24 (emphasis original).
48. Present volume, 103–104.
49. Present volume, 107.
50. J. T. Beck, *Erklärung des Briefes Pauli an die Epheser: Nebst Anmerkungen zum Brief Pauli an die Kolosser* (Gütersloh: Bertelsman, 1891).
51. Present volume, 107.
52. Present volume, 108.
53. Present volume, 128.
54. Present volume, 129 (emphasis original).
55. Present volume, 129.
56. Present volume, 129.
57. Present volume, 129.
58. Present volume, 65.
59. Present volume, 65.
60. Present volume, 65–66.
61. Present volume, 66.
62. Present volume, 66.
63. Present volume, 67.
64. Present volume, 67.
65. Present volume, 67.
66. Present volume, 67 (emphasis original).
67. Present volume, 68.
68. Present volume, 68.
69. Present volume, 68–69 (emphasis original).

**Exposition of Ephesians, Winter Semester 1921–22**

1. "It is doubtful," a legal term used when there is not sufficient evidence to decide the case. Here Barth follows Adolf Jülicher, who argues that Pauline authorship of Ephesians is unlikely. See Jülicher, *An Introduction to the New Testament*, trans. Janet Penrose Ward (New York: G. P. Putnam's Sons, 1904), 142–47.
2. Martin Dibelius, *An die Epheser*, in *Die Briefe des Apostels Paulus II: Die neun kleinen Briefe*, Handbuch zum Neuen Testament 3/2 (Tübingen: J. C. B. Mohr, 1913), 113–14.
3. Adolf Jülicher, *Einleitung in das Neue Testament*, 6. Aufl., Grundriss der theologischen Wissenschaften 3/1 (Tübingen/Leipzig: J. C. B. Mohr, 1921), 120–28; → ET, Jülicher, *Introduction to the New Testament*, 127–47.
4. Fritz Barth, *Einleitung in das Neue Testament*, 5. Aufl. (Gütersloh: C. Bertelsmann 1921), 74–81.

5. Henrich Julius Holtzmann, *Lehrbuch der historisch-kritischen Einleitung in das Neue Testament*, 3. Aufl. (Freiburg im Breisgau: J. C. B. Mohr, 1892), 257–66, especially 265.

6. Barth's suggestion and wording here bear a strong resemblance to Fritz Barth's handling of the subject. See F. Barth, *Einleitung*, 78. See also B. Weiß, *Lehrbuch der Einleitung in das Neue Testament*, 3. Aufl. (Berlin: W. Hertz, 1897), 252–53; Jülicher, *Einleitung*, 127–28.

7. Dibelius, *An die Epheser*, 113–14.

8. This statement reflects Barth's experience. He began serious exegetical work on Ephesians shortly after producing a small commentary on 1 Corinthians in November 1919. See Eberhard Busch, *Karl Barth: His Life from Letters and Autobiographical Texts*, trans. John Bowden (Grand Rapids: Eerdmans, 1994), 108.

9. For the term *hieratischen*, translated here as "ceremonial," see Paul Wendland, *Die urchristlichen Literaturformen*, 3. Aufl., Handbuch zum Neuen Testament 1/3 (Tübingen: J. C. B. Mohr, 1912), 364; Dibelius, *An die Epheser*, 97. The term "solemn" appears in Jülicher's *Introduction*: the Pauline thanksgivings are distinguished by "a solemn contemplation of the majesty which, through Christ, had given mankind the Gospel of atonement, of re-creation and of peace" (*Introduction*, 129).

10. Henrich Julius Holtzmann, *Lehrbuch der Neutestamentlichen Theologie* (Tübingen: Mohr Siebeck, 1911), 1: 226–51; Wendland, *Literaturformen*, 364.

11. Holtzmann, *Theologie*, 1:240–45; cf. 1:250.

12. See ibid., 1:236.

13. See ibid., 1:257.

14. Ibid.

15. See F. Barth, *Einleitung*, 78; Jülicher, *Einleitung*, 5.6, 1:120–28.

16. Barth is thinking primarily about the mystical leanings and the Pythagorean tendencies of the older Plato.

17. On the matter of the "metamorphosis" of Friedrich Wilhelm Joseph von Schelling (1775–1854), Holtzman suggests in a note an alternative way of assessing the authorship question; his observation occurs in the wider context of questions about Pauline authorship, which he rejects.

18. Paul Natorp (1854–1924), professor of philosophy and pedagogy at Marburg. Natorp was one of the neo-Kantian thinkers who may have influenced Barth during this period. For a discussion, see Bruce L. McCormack, *Karl Barth's Critically Realistic Dialectical Theology: Its Genesis and Development 1909–1936* (Oxford: Oxford University Press, 1997), 160–62.

19. Holtzmann, *Theologie*, 1:227; Dibelius, *An die Epheser*, 113.

20. "Do not ask: Who wrote it? but: What is written?" The editor of the German edition notes that the existence of this sentence cannot be confirmed in the writings of Johann Albrecht Bengel.

21. Here Barth follows Fritz Barth. See F. Barth, *Einleitung*, 75.

22. "In classical Greek, the word apostolos refers to a fleet expedition [maneuver] or its leader, the admiral" (Hans Lietzmann, *Einführung in die Textgeschichte*

*der Paulusbriefe: An die Römer*, Handbuch zum Neuen Testament 3 [Tübingen: Mohr Siebeck: 1919], 24).

23. "Now about the apostles and prophets: Act in line with the gospel precept. Welcome every apostle on arriving, as if he were the Lord. But he must not stay beyond one day. In case of necessity, however, the next day too. If he stays three days, he is a false prophet. On departing, an apostle must not accept anything save sufficient food to carry him till his next lodging" ("The Teaching of the Twelve Apostles, Commonly Called the Didache," trans. Cyril C. Richardson, in *Early Christian Fathers*, Library of Christian Classics 1 [Philadelphia: Westminster: 1953], 176).

24. Lietzmann, *Einführung*, 23.

25. "Apostolic calling is a paradoxical factor which from first to last in his life stands paradoxically outside his personal identity with himself as the definite person he is" (Søren Kierkegaard, "Of the Difference between a Genius and an Apostle," trans. Alexander Dru, in *The Present Age and Two Minor Ethico-Religious Treatises* [London: Oxford University Press, 1940], 143).

26. German: *unmittelbares*. With this term Barth refers to psychologically quantifiable knowledge that is available without mediation. "Unmediated" conveys Barth's meaning better than the standard translation "immediate." "The German terms 'mittelbar' and 'unmittelbar' translate as 'mediate' and 'immediate,' where the German emphasis is upon the 'medium,' that which 'mediates.' Although this root idea is still present in the English terms, it is largely lost in current usage" (Karl Barth, *The Theology of the Reformed Confessions, 1923*, trans. Darrell L. Guder and Judith J. Guder [Louisville: John Knox, 2002], 286). For a discussion of Barth's use of the term, see McCormack, *Critically Realistic Dialectical Theology*, 160–62.

27. German: *seine Sache*.

28. "An Apostle is what he is through having divine authority. *Divine authority* is, *qualitatively*, *the decisive factor*" (Kierkegaard, "A Genius and an Apostle," 144 [emphasis original]).

29. "The uniting of opposites."

30. Cf. Rom. 1:16, which includes the phrase δύναμις . . . θεοῦ.

31. German: *nicht sein Erlebnis, seine Erfahrung*; alternately: "not his personal experience or empirical experience."

32. John Calvin, *Sermons on the Epistle to the Ephesians*, trans. Arthur Golding (Edinburgh: Banner of Truth Trust, 1973), 11–12. In the manuscript, Barth includes this entire passage, but he alternates between German and the original French for emphasis:

> For one of the common artifices which the devil uses to diminish reverence for God's Word is to place before our eyes the person who brings it. "Or il est certain que nous sommes des vaisseaux *fragiles* et de *nulle* valeur, voire mesmes comme des pots cassez." What is there in those whom God has ordained to be the ministers of his Word? But the treasure is inestimably great at all times, despite the contemptibleness of the vessels [2 Cor.

4:7]. "Notons bien donc, quand les *hommes* viennent à nous pour estre tesmoins de la remission de nos pechez et du salut qu'il nous faut esperer, que nostre foy doit monter *plus* haut, et qu'il n'est pas question de nous enquerir, *et* cestuy-ci merite-il d'estre escouté? Et *qui* est-il en sa personne? Contentons-nous que *Dieu* par ce moyen-là nous veut attirer à *soy*."

33. For similar use of this expression, see Karl Barth, *The Epistle to the Romans*, trans. Edwyn C. Hoskyns (London: Oxford University Press, 1968), 29, 36, 65. This passage is an example of how Barth adapted terminology from Franz Overbeck's *Christentum und Kultur*. For a discussion, see McCormack, *Critically Realistic Dialectical Theology*, 232.

34. "Good pleasure." In Reformed theology, the phrase is particularly associated with "the ground of God's elective choice (Eph. 1:5) . . . where emphasis is placed on the freedom and sovereignty of the divine purpose" (Richard A. Muller, *Dictionary of Latin and Greek Theological Terms: Drawn Principally from Protestant and Scholastic Theology* [Grand Rapids: Baker, 1985], 57).

35. When Barth distinguishes here between miracle (*Mirakel*) and wonder (*Wunder*), the latter refers to a divine event that occurs within contingent reality. Describing the devolution of the doctrine of verbal inspiration, Barth says: "The divine wonder of inspiration became the worldly wonder of inspiredness. To put it differently, the wonder [*Wunder*] became a miracle [*Mirakel*] that then as such quite rightly had to evoke reservations, criticism, and laughter" (*Theology of the Reformed Confessions*, 62). However, Barth does not maintain the distinction consistently. Sometimes when he says *Mirakel*, he clearly means "miracle." The context determines which meaning is in view.

36. Søren Kierkegaard, *Philosophische Brocken: Abschließende unwissenschaftliche Nachschrift*, Erster Teil, übers. H. Gottsched und Chr. Schrempf, Gesammelte Werke 6 (Jena: E. Diederichs, 1910), 209.

37. "For what is infinite cannot be spoken of too much" (John Calvin, *The Epistles of Paul the Apostle to the Galatians, Ephesians, Philippians and Colossians*, trans. T. H. L. Parker, Calvin's New Testament Commentaries [Grand Rapids: Eerdmans, 1965], 133).

38. In certain games, "Rechenpfennige" serve as temporary payment of winnings. The sentence could be translated: "Because faith is a human action, we must guard against treating it like a counting token that needs to be redistributed once and again. We have only one faith to distribute, and it is a *res infinita*."

39. Barth misreads Jerome here. Jerome considers then rejects the suggestion that "those who are saints and faithful in Ephesus are referred to by the term 'being.'" He mentions interpreters who support this reading on the basis of Exod. 3:14, "He who is has sent me," and concludes that they are "more curious than is necessary." Jerome favors the theory that it was "written straightforwardly not to those 'who are,' but 'who are the saints and faithful in Ephesus.'" See Ronald E. Heine, ed., *The Commentaries of Origen and Jerome on St Paul's Epistle to the Ephesians*, Oxford Early Christian Studies (Oxford: Oxford University Press, 2002), 80.

40. This is Jülicher's position; see Jülicher, *Introduction*, 140–42.

41. Heinrich A. W. Meyer, *Critical and Exegetical Hand-Book to the Epistle to the Ephesians*, trans. Maurice J. Evans, rev. and ed. William P. Dickson, Meyer Commentary on the New Testament 7 (New York: Funk & Wagnalls, 1884), 287–350.

42. Johann Albrecht Bengel, *Gnomon of the New Testament*, vol. 4, trans. James Bryce, rev. and ed. Andrew Fausset (Edinburgh: T&T Clark, 1858), 61–62.

43. Hermann Olshausen, *Biblical Commentary on the New Testament*, vol. 4, trans. David Fosdick Jr. (New York: Sheldon, Blakeman, 1857–58).

44. "Tychicus I have sent to Ephesus" (2 Tim. 4:12). Dibelius, *An die Epheser*, 96.

45. Cf. Rom. 1:8; 1 Cor. 1:4; Phil. 1:3; 1 Thess. 1:2; Philem. 4.

46. "The hidden God is the revealed God." According to Richard A. Muller, these two expressions convey "the paradox of God's unknowability and self-manifestation as stated by Luther. . . . God is revealed in his hiddenness and hidden in his revelation" (*Dictionary of Latin and Greek Theological Terms*, 90).

47. Cf. Barth, *Theology of the Reformed Confessions*, 56–57: "With the statement, 'It is God's Word!' we have arrived apparently at the point where the scriptural principle seems to be grounded on its groundlessness, or better, it is grounded in God alone."

48. To give honor to God alone is a theme in the theology of John Calvin. See Calvin's *Institutes* (1550), I/2.

49. German: *mit*. "Grace be with you and peace from God our Father and from the Lord Jesus Christ!" (Eph. 1:2, Luther's translation).

50. Barth attributes this idea to Calvin. See Karl Barth, *The Theology of John Calvin*, trans. Geoffrey W. Bromiley (Grand Rapids: Eerdmans, 1995), 80.

51. German: *das Gnädige der Gnade*.

52. Cf. *Goethe's Faust: The Original German and a New Translation and Introduction by Walter Kaufmann* (Garden City: Anchor, 1963), part 2, act 5, scene 7, lines 12106–9 (pp. 502–3):

CHORUS MYSTICUS:
What is destructible
Is but a parable;
What fails ineluctably,
The undeclarable,
Here it was seen,
Here it was action.

53. German: *sachgemäß*.

54. The idea is expressed by Barth in *Romans*: precisely because this distance is acknowledged, the distance or separation becomes the basis for proximity or closeness.

55. Friedrich Schleiermacher, *The Christian Faith*, trans. H. R. Mackintosh and J. S. Stewart (Edinburgh: T&T Clark, 1928–56), 16.

56. The phrase "the thought about God" occurs frequently in Barth's writings during this period. For another example, see Barth, *Theology of the Reformed Confessions*, 110.

57. Cf. Barth, *Romans*, 151; John Calvin: "The true conviction which believers have of the word of God, of their own salvation, and of all religion, does not spring from the feeling of the flesh, or from human and philosophical arguments, but from the sealing of the Spirit, who makes their consciences more certain and removes all doubt" (*Galatians, Ephesians, Philippians and Colossians*, 131).

58. For other examples of this signature phrase, see Barth, *Romans*, 11, 83, 346; Barth, *The Göttingen Dogmatics: Instruction in the Christian Religion*, vol. 1, ed. Hannelotte Reiffen, trans. Geoffrey W. Bromiley (Grand Rapids: Eerdmans, 1991), 88. See also the discussion in Eberhard Jüngel, "Barth's Theological Beginnings," chapter 2 in *Karl Barth: A Theological Legacy*, trans. Garrett E. Paul (Philadelphia: Westminster, 1986).

59. It is not clear which of the two Blumhardts Barth has in mind here. In this context, he could mean Christoph Blumhardt (1842–1919), pastor and leader of the Bad Boll community, which Barth visited in April 1915. Blumhardt's meditation "Peace Be with You" impressed Barth on that visit. See Eberhard Busch, *Karl Barth: His Life from Letters and Autobiographical Texts*, trans. John Bowden (Grand Rapids: Eerdmans, 1994), 85. For Barth's meditation on Blumhardt following Blumhardt's death, August 2, 1919, see Karl Barth, *Predigten, 1919*, hg. Hermann Schmidt, GA 39 (Zürich: TVZ, 2003), 291–95.

60. "Then he said to them, 'Give to the emperor the things that are the emperor's, and to God the things that are God's'" (Matt. 22:21).

61. "For what is infinite cannot be spoken of too much" (Calvin, *Epistles of Paul*, 133).

62. The concept of the *Ursprung* ("origin") is a dominant theme in Barth's early theology. For examples, see Barth, *Romans*, 342, 346; idem, "The Christian's Place in Society," in *The Word of God and the Word of Man*, trans. Douglas Horton (London: Hodder & Stoughton, 1928), 285.

63. "God has blessed us in one sense, we bless Him in another" (Bengel, *Gnomon of the New Testament*, 63).

64. In Hegelian terminology, the term "sublation" (*Aufhebung*) and cognates could be translated "abrogation" or "suppression," but given Hegel's special usage, "sublation" is the best choice. According to Charles Taylor, "In Hegel's special usage, the term combines its ordinary meaning with a rarer sense of 'setting aside' or 'preservation.' It thus serves to designate the dialectical transition in which a lower state is both cancelled and preserved in a higher" (*Hegel* [Cambridge: Cambridge University Press, 1975], xi).

65. See Calvin's comments on 1:3 in *Sermons on the Epistle to the Ephesians*, Sermon 1, 15–21; cf. idem, *Galatians, Ephesians, Philippians and Colossians*, 123–24.

66. Dibelius, *An die Epheser*, 99. Barth accurately summarizes Dibelius's outline, which divides the passage into distinct sections, beginning with the phrase,

"in Christ" or "in him." Dibelius groups vv. 4–6, vv. 7–10, and vv. 11–12 and vv. 12–13, although his schema is not quite as clearly delineated as Barth's outline.

67. German: *so einheitlich, so beweglich*.

68. Barth's translation emphasizes the compelling nature of Paul's experience. "Obligation" (*Zwang*) suggests pressure, an irresistible urge, or an impulse rather than a legal obligation.

69. Calvin, *Sermons on the Epistle to the Ephesians*, Sermon 1, 20.

70. A reference to Paul in Athens, where the apostle speaks of "the unknown god."

71. "To begin at the beginning" is a signature Barthian phrase from the early period to the very end. See Karl Barth, *Predigten, 1916*, hg. Hermann Schmidt, GA 29 (Zürich: TVZ, 1998), 118; idem, *Evangelical Theology: An Introduction* (New York: Holt, Rinehart, and Winston, 1963), 165.

72. "Learned ignorance," i.e., prescribed or acquired lack of knowledge.

73. "Infused grace."

74. The editor of the critical edition inserts *bezeichnet* (from *bezeichnen*, "to denote") in brackets to complete the statement.

75. Cf. the controversy over the demand for "simplicity" in the preface to Barth, *Romans*, 5–6.

76. This comment anticipates Barth's polemical response to Harnack in 1923, when he repeatedly criticizes Harnack for speaking of the "simple gospel" ("schlichte Evangelium") and for portraying Paul as complicated, dogmatic, and systematic in contrast to the simple Jesus. What Harnack calls the "simple Gospel," Barth argues, is "what is left over" when the Bible's subject matter, i.e., revelation, is removed. Barth concludes that "neither revelation nor faith is made understandable in the familiar 'simple' way as a frame of mind" that Harnack advocates. See Karl Barth, "An Professor Dr. Adolf von Harnack, Berlin, 1923," in *Offene Briefe 1909–1935*, hg. Diether Koch, GA 35 (Zürich: TVZ, 2001), 55–88; → ET, "The Debate on the Critical Historical Method: Correspondence between Adolf von Harnack and Karl Barth," in *The Beginnings of Dialectic Theology*, vol. 1, ed. James M. Robinson, trans. Keith R. Crim (Richmond: John Knox, 1968), 165–87, especially 177, 185.

77. Cf. Barth, *Romans*, 38: "'Now, Spirit is the denial of direct immediacy. If Christ be very God, He must be unknown, for to be known directly is the characteristic mark of an idol' (Kierkegaard)."

78. German: *Plerophorie*, from the Greek πλήρωμα (Eph. 1:10): "the state of being full, fullness of time." See *A Greek-English Lexicon of the New Testament and Other Early Christian Literature*, rev. and ed. Frederick William Danker, 3rd ed. (Chicago: University of Chicago Press, 2000), s.v. "πλήρωμα."

79. Cf. Barth, *Romans*, 38.

80. The emphasis and exclamation mark are Barth's. Luther's translation has a hortatory element, which is lacking in the English: "Lass dir an meiner Gnade genügen" ("Let my grace be sufficient for you"), *Die Lutherbibel*, 2 Cor. 12:9.

81. Calvin frequently speaks about "robbing" God when we attribute to ourselves what is rightly God's. See, e.g., the following passage from Calvin's commentary on Galatians: "Therefore, let us assure ourselves that we hold all things of God and his pure grace, and that we cannot attribute anything to ourselves, unless we intend to rob him of his right" (*Galatians and Ephesians*, 12).

82. Alternately: "the ultimate dissolution and reconstituting of my own existence."

83. An allusion to Luke 9:24.

84. The German critical edition includes in brackets the phrase *muss man sagen*, "it must be said."

85. German: *Regressus*, i.e., by imagining God's creative activity as a superior form of human creativity.

86. Barth refers here to Faust's famous revision of the Johannine prologue. See Johann Wolfgang von Goethe, *Faust: A Tragedy*, trans. Walter Arndt, ed. Cyrus Hamlin, 2nd ed. (New York: Norton, 2001), part 1, "Study," lines 1224–37 (p. 34).

87. Cf. Dibelius, *An die Epheser*, 97.

88. Paul "only wanted to express the superiority of that grace which is bestowed on us through Christ" (Calvin, *Galatians, Ephesians, Philippians and Colossians*, 124).

89. J. C. K. von Hofmann, *Der Brief Pauli an die Epheser* (Nördlingen: Beck, 1870), 8.

90. In Barth's manuscript, there is a cross-reference here to his earlier discussion of ἐν Χριστῷ in his December 1 lecture.

91. See Calvin's comments in *Sermons on the Epistle to the Ephesians*, Sermon 2, 25–34.

92. Hofmann, *Epheser*, 9.

93. Albrecht Ritschl, *Die christliche Lehre der Rechtfertigung und Versöhnung*, 3. Bd., *Die positive Entwickelung der Lehre* (Bonn: Marcus, 1895[4]), 123.

94. J. T. Beck, *Erklärung des Briefes Pauli an die Epheser: Nebst Anmerkungen zum Brief Pauli an die Kolosser* (Gütersloh: Bertelsman, 1891), 44–45.

95. Philipp Matthäus Hahn, *Erbauungs-Stunden über den Brief an die Epheser* (Basel: Ferd. Riehm, 1878[4]), 7–8.

96. Erich Haupt, *Der Brief an die Epheser*, in *Die Gefangenschaftsbriefe*, Bd. 8/9, *Kritisch-exegetischer Kommentar über das Neue Testament*, 6. Aufl (Göttingen: Vandenhoeck und Ruprecht, 1902), 7.

97. See, e.g., the beginning of *Sermons on the Epistle to the Ephesians*, Sermon 3, where Calvin comments, "I began to show you . . ." The labor of explaining double predestination took up the entire second sermon and the first part of the third.

98. ". . . such great profit from it that it had been much better if we had never been born than be ignorant of what St. Paul shows here . . . it were better that the whole world should go to confusion than that this doctrine should be reduced to silence" (Calvin, *Sermons on the Epistle to the Ephesians*, 26). The French has been reproduced as it appeared in Barth's manuscript.

99. See Rom. 9:14–26, where Paul speaks of God's decision to harden certain hearts and to bear with "patience the objects of his wrath."

100. One of Barth's favorite images is the prominent pointing finger of John the Baptist in the *Isenheim Altarpiece*. There, John's finger points up to the crucified and dying Christ. See Barth, "Biblical Questions, Insights and Vistas," in *The Word of God and the Word of Man*, 65.

101. "The profit of this doctrine." Barth attributes this phrase to Calvin, but in fact he has created it by combining words from the following sentence: "Au reste, il y a deux raisons pour monstrer qu'il est plus que necessaire que ceste doctrine se presche, et que nous en avons une utilité si grande" (Calvin, *Sermons sur L'épître aux Éphésiens*, 262 [ET, *Sermons on the Epistle to the Ephesians*, 26: "But there are yet two more reasons which show that this doctrine must of necessity be preached, and that we reap such great profit from it"]).

102. A reference to Ps. 90:3. Cf. "Biblical Questions," 78–79, where Barth says that this psalm expresses the "unmistakable undertone of the piety of the Psalms which people so much admire."

103. German: *Einzelnheit und Einsamkeit*. The word *Einsamkeit* suggests isolation and solitude. Barth's meaning is clarified by noting how he uses a similar word, *Isoliertheit*, to speak of God's complete majesty and freedom: "God speaks—and as we say this, we must always hear God in his superiority, his majesty and freedom, in his isolatedness as God" (*Theology of the Reformed Confessions*, 56). It is notable that here he applies the same term to Jesus Christ as he does to humanity, a move that is consistent with his concern to show the relation between divine and human existence.

104. "For if we are chosen *in* Christ, it is *outside* ourselves" (Calvin, *Galatians, Ephesians, Philippians and Colossians*, 125). Barth omits "Nam" and repeats "sumus electi" ("*we are chosen*") for emphasis.

105. German: *Einzigen*.

106. Beck, *Epheser*, 49.

107. Haupt, *Der Brief an die Epheser*, 9.

108. Hermann von Soden, *Die Briefe an die Kolosser, Epheser, Philemon; die Pastoralbriefe* (Freiburg: Mohr Siebeck, 1893), 107.

109. German: *auf der ganzen Linie Erschütterter und aus der Bahn Geworfener*. Literally: "shaken down the line and thrown off track." The closest English idiom for the first phrase is "across the boards." But Barth is playing with the image of a train or tram being pitched while moving down the track and then derailed.

110. "The glory of God is the highest end, to which our sanctification is subordinate" (Calvin, *Galatians, Ephesians, Philippians and Colossians*, 125).

111. "Highest end."

112. German: *daß Gott für uns eintritt*, taking *eintreten für* to mean "stand up for someone" or "speak in someone's defense" in the legal sense.

113. German: *diesen objektiven, sozusagen juristischen Eigenschaften des Menschen*. By this phrase, Barth means the holiness and blamelessness that are

declared by God rather than any ethical qualities that we might possess. The phrase is difficult to translate, since the English expression "human characteristics" sounds like something we possess, which is contrary to Barth's meaning.

114. Cf. Barth, *Romans*, 157–58.

115. German: *Faktizität.*

116. German: *Einkindung.* Haupt, *Der Brief an die Epheser*, 9.

117. German: *weder geschaffen noch gezeugt.*

118. German: *Gottesfremden* ("estranged from God"); *Gotteskindern* ("children of God").

119. Barth uses *gegenüber* idiosyncratically here, i.e., as a noun to refer to Jesus Christ, who is appointed by God *gegunüber der Totalität des uns bekannten Lebenszusammenhangs als das Gegenüber, das eben nur Gott geben kann.*

120. Dibelius, *An die Epheser*, 98.

121. NRSV; alternately: "that which is well pleasing." Barth uses *Wohlgefallen* to translate the Greek *eudokia.*

122. "God embraces us in His love and favour freely and not on a wages basis"; and "in adopting us, therefore, the Lord does not look at what we are, and is not reconciled to us by any personal worth. His single motive is the eternal good pleasure, by which He predestinated us" (Calvin, *Galatians, Ephesians, Philippians and Colossians*, 127).

123. "This is the true fountain from which we must draw our knowledge of the divine mercy" (*Galatians, Ephesians, Philippians and Colossians*, 126).

124. German: *Will-Kür.*

125. German: *die Logik der Sache.*

126. Cf. Barth, *Romans*, 104–5.

127. Beck, *Epheser*, 62.

128. German: *Belebtheit.*

129. German: *Weisheit* ("wisdom"); *Klugheit* ("insight").

130. Beck, *Epheser*, 68–69.

131. German: *Weltwirklichkeit.*

132. German: *Göttlich Notwendigen.* This could otherwise be rendered as: "the unheard of fact of the divine vulnerability to this-world reality" or "the unprecedented event in which God makes himself a necessary part of this world."

133. German: *Zufälligkeit.*

134. Not even this moment (of Jesus) qualifies—i.e., as something that can be known indirectly.

135. The "diffuse elements."

136. Selma Lagerlöf, "In the Temple," in *Christ Legends*, trans. Velma Swanston Howard (New York: Henry Holt, 1908), 95–118. In the story, two pillars called "Righteousness' Gate" stood "so close to each other that hardly a straw could be squeezed in between them" (103). In order to rescue a poor widow from an unscrupulous judge in the temple, Jesus performs a miracle: "He put his shoulder in the groove between the two pillars, as if to make a way. . . . That instant [Righteousness' Gate] . . . rumbled in the vaults, and it sang in the old

pillars, and they glided apart— one to the right and one to the left—and made a space wide enough for the boy's slender body to pass between them!" (108).

137. German: *Denkvorgang*.

138. "For what is the analogy (*proportio*) between the creature and the Creator, without the interposition of the Mediator?" (*Galatians, Ephesians, Philippians and Colossians*, 129).

139. Following Dibelius, *An die Epheser*, 98; cf. Eberhard Nestle, *Novum Testamentum Graece cum apparatu critico ex editionibus et libris manu scriptis collecto* (Stuttgart: Privilegierte Württembergische Bibelanstalt, 1898, 1899, 1901). The Nestle text reads as follows: εἰς οἰκονομίαν τοῦ πληρώματος τῶν καιρῶν, ἀνακεφαλαιώσασθαι τὰ πάντα ἐν τῷ Χριστῷ, τὰ ἐπὶ τοῖς οὐρανοῖς καὶ τὰ ἐπὶ τῆς γῆς | ἐν αὐτῷ, ἐν ᾧ καὶ ἐκληρώθημεν προορισθέντες κατὰ πρόθεσιν τοῦ τὰ πάντα ἐνεργοῦντος κατὰ τὴν βουλὴν τοῦ θελήματος αὐτοῦ. The vertical line in the phrase ἐπὶ τῆς γῆς | ἐν αὐτῷ has been added to indicate the crucial transition from v. 10 to v. 11 that Barth has in mind.

140. That is, in contrast to the ἐν αὐτῷ in v. 11, which would not be obviously grammatically connected to Christ.

141. To have the future "as future" is a dialectical expression, conveying the paradox that the future is already actual in the life of the believer and yet still in the form of promise.

142. German: *Bestimmungen . . . als Wartende, als Hoffende*. This is a characteristic phrase of Barth's, suggesting God's sovereign determination to make us who we are. Literally, "It designates them, in contrast to the determinations in vv. 7–10 as the ones who wait, as the ones who hope."

143. Hofmann, *Epheser*, 23–24.

144. Beck, *Epheser*, 3, 82–83.

145. Meyer, *Critical and Exegetical Hand-Book*, 327. According to Meyer: "ἐκληρώθημεν means: *we were made partakers of the* κλῆρος, 'inheritance' (Acts 26:18; Col. 1:12), that is, *of the possession of the Messianic kingdom*, which before the Parousia is an ideal possession (v. 14; Rom. 8:24), and thereafter a real one."

146. See Johann Wolfgang von Goethe, *Egmont*, act 3, scene 2 (ET, *Goethe's Plays*, trans. Charles E. Passage [New York: Frederick Ungar, 1980], 333).

Sky high exulting
To death burdened down;
Happiness lives
In the lover alone.

See also Barth, *Theology of the Reformed Confessions*, 123: "Where that does happen, Christianity cannot help but land on the 'escalator' [*trottoir roulant*] of emotional experiences, up in that 'sky high exulting,' before which the soul that *loves* God is not protected and must therefore be defended."

147. "Self-regulated, or rather, regulated by God." Literally, "the Christian is *a law unto himself* or rather, *by God's law*." In the first case, Barth is stressing that the Christian is autonomous or independent of the forces that go up and

down. In the second phrase, he qualifies this statement, using a play on words to say that the Christian is not independent of God but rather lives by his command. The translation "self-regulated . . . divine-regulated" is an attempt to express the play on words.

148. Cf. Barth, *Romans*, 208: "But I am also disturbed, for the demand bids me take up arms against the world of men and against the men of the world."

149. Beck, *Epheser*, 86.

150. Bengel, *Gnomon of the New Testament*, 68–69.

151. Meyer, *Critical and Exegetical Hand-Book*, 328–30.

152. Von Soden, *Epheser*, 111.

153. Dibelius, *An die Epheser*, 99.

154. Barth seems to be saying that by virtue of addressing the Ephesian Christians as σφραγισθέντες ("those who are sealed by the Spirit"), he touches the objective point in them; he simultaneously addresses them ad hominem, ἐν ᾧ καὶ ὑμεῖς ("in you also"), touching the subjective point in them and therefore the point where the objective εὐλογία πνευματική (v. 3) is revealed as subjective (where subjective and the objective are one).

155. German: *durchschauen*. The word means to "see through," or "to see things as they really are." In order to emphasize the theme of penetrating or breaking through beyond the surface of things, which is implicit in Barth's argument, this sentence could be translated: "the more clearly we see through the relativity of all things." Cf. James 1:25, *Lutherbibel*: "*Wer aber durchschaut in das vollkommene Gesetz der Freheit. . . .*"

156. German: *In ihm ist das Nicht-Gegebene gegeben, Gott offenbar*. Alternately: "In him, the noncontingent becomes contingent."

157. German: *Was die Genitive sagen, das tritt real ein mit dem, was das Hauptwort sagt*. Barth means that the announcement *about* salvation actually occasions salvation.

158. John Calvin, *Commentarius in Epistolam Sancti Pauli Ad Ephesos*, 154; → ET: Paul's "frequent mention of the glory of God ought not to be thought superfluous, for what is infinite cannot be spoken of too much. This is particularly true in commending the Divine mercy, to whose meaning no godly person will ever be able to do justice in words. All godly tongues will be as ready to utter His praises as their ears will be open to hear them. For if men and angels combined their eloquence on this theme, it would still fall far short of its greatness" (*Galatians, Ephesians, Philippians and Colossians*, 133).

159. Karl Barth's translation.

160. Bengel, *Gnomon of the New Testament*, 257; "a compendium of the gospel."

161. Cf. Karl Barth and Eduard Thurneysen, *Revolutionary Theology in the Making: Barth-Thurneysen Correspondence, 1914–1925*, trans. James D. Smart (Richmond: John Knox, 1964), 43: "Paul—what a man he must have been, and what men also those for whom he could so sketch and hint at these pithy things in a few muddled fragments!"

162. Alternately: "I hope that I have convinced you that it is possible to stand with Paul, to perceive what he perceives, and not only to see along with him but to think along with him from that point where the subject matter. . . ."

163. Barth means that one finds oneself only when life is seen from the apex, i.e., life lived to the praise of the glory of God. Because other believers have made the same discovery, it becomes a ligament that binds them to one another, even though this bond may be restricting or quite elastic in other respects.

164. Alternately: "He begins again at the beginning," one of Barth's signature phrases.

165. German: *Da ist nichts schon im Werden order gar im Sein*. In other words, nothing exists in and of itself; it has existence only in relation to God. Cf. Karl Barth, *Witness to the Word: A Commentary on John 1 by Karl Barth, Lectures at Münster in 1925 and at Bonn in 1933*, ed. Walther Fürst, trans. Geoffrey W. Bromiley (Grand Rapids: Eerdmans, 1986), 34, where Barth employs similar language in his discussion of "*egeneto*" in John 1:3: "Everything that has come into being is completely different from him. . . . This is how things are with all that is. It is related to God. It is something and not nothing. But it is something only as it is related to the Word. Its existence is conceivable only in the light of the Word."

166. "For nothing is more dangerous than satiety of spiritual benefits" (Calvin, *Galatians, Ephesians, Philippians and Colossians*, 134).

167. "God as he really is"; or, "We must call upon God, acknowledging that he alone is God."

168. German: *der Kämpfer um Gott*. Barth uses *Kämpfe*r and its cognates to describe someone who is faithful to the truth of the gospel. Cf. Barth, *Die Theologie der Reformierten Bekenntnisschriften*, GA 30 (Zürich: TVZ, 1998), 136 (→ ET, *Theology of the Reformed Confessions*, 86), where grace is described as that which "inevitably makes a person into a worker and a fighter [die den Menschen unweigerlich zum Arbeiter und Kämpfer macht]." See also *Die Theologie der Reformierten Bekenntnisschriften*, 86 (*Theology of the Reformed Confessions*, 78), where Barth speaks of the "der Richtung des reformierten *Kampfes*" and of Zwingli's Geneva confession as a "*Kampf*document" (Barth's emphases).

169. "Order of salvation."

170. German: *was not tut, ineinander in der lebendigen Bewegung*. For a discussion of the *ineinander* relationship of time and eternity, which appears frequently in Barth, *Romans* I, see McCormack, *Critically Realistic Dialectical Theology*, 144–46.

171. German: *ihr müßt die Fähigkeit gebrauchen, über dieses Eurige hinaus euch immer wider aufzuschleißen für den Gegenstand*. I have substituted visual images where Barth uses spatial metaphors; he is saying that on the basis of what they already have, they are to proceed; and yet any advance is toward the subject that is ahead of them. This idea is consistent with Barth's overall theme that God's blessings are the source and the goal of human existence.

172. Barth was given access to Franz Overbeck's archives by Overbeck's student Carl Albrecht Bernoulli. Upon reading Overbeck's *Christentum und Kultur: Gedanken und Anmerkungen zur modernen Theologie* (Basel: Benno Schwabe, 1919); Kritische Neuausgabe: Franz Overbeck, *Werke und Nachlaß*, Bd. 6/1, *Kirchenlexicon Materialien: Christentum und Kultur*, hg. Barbara von Reibnitz (Stuttgart; Weimar: Metzler, 1966), Barth wrote a lengthy review essay (Barth, *Unerledigte Anfragen an die heutige Theologie* [1920]; reprinted in *Die Theologie und Kirche* [Munich: Kaiser Verlag, 1928], 2.8, 1–25) in which he summarizes Overbeck's criticism of modern Christianity, namely, that it has drifted so far from early Christianity that its central claims simply mirror modern thought. As such, "the essence of modern Christianity [is] its insignificance" (see Barth, *Unerledigte Anfragen*, 15; cf. Overbeck, *Christentum und Kultur* [*Kirchenlexicon Materialien*, 100f.]). Overbeck himself remarked of Chateaubriand's *Génie du christianisme* and Harnack's *Wesen des Christentums*: "Both works would be better understood if given the title *The Insignificance of Christianity*, or perhaps *The Spirit of Christianity in My Time*" (Overbeck, *Christentum und Kultur*, 67–68 [*Kirchenlexicon Materialien*, 100–101]).

173. "Par excellence."

174. For a discussion of Barth's mature thinking on time and eternity, see George Hunsinger, "*Mysterium Trinitatis*: Karl Barth's Doctrine of the Holy Spirit," in *Disruptive Grace: Studies in the Theology of Karl Barth* (Grand Rapids: Eerdmans, 2000), 186–209.

175. The paradoxical nature of questions and answers is a frequent theme in Barth's writings of the period. For other examples, see "The Strange New World of the Bible," in *The Word of God and the Word of Man*, 28–50, especially 32, 39, 43; note also "Biblical Questions," 53: "The question we ask becomes a question asked of us."

176. Barth is saying that even if Paul's account is superior to other accounts by a factor of 1,000 to 1, the relationship or degree of accuracy of the Pauline account to the event itself is 1,000 to infinity.

177. Cf. the Socratic motto: "He who thinks that he knows, knows not. But he who knows that he knows not is the one who knows."

178. German: *Seid ihr, was ihr seid?* Cf. Barth, *Romans*, 207, where he quotes Godet: "Be what thou already art in Christ."

179. The "waiting that hastens" is a prominent theme in Barth's theology during this period. See Barth, *Romans*, 157, 183.

180. German: *die scheidende Mitte*. Cf. Barth, *Romans*, 195, where he says that "*the life hid with Christ in God* (Col. 3:1) . . . is the invisible point of observation and of relationship, the judgment exercised by my infinite upon my finite existence; it is the threatening and promising which is set beyond time, beyond all visibility, beyond all the finite and concrete events of my life."

181. ET: Gotthold Ephraim Lessing, "On the Proof of the Spirit and of Power," in *Lessing's Theological Writings*, trans. H. Chadwick (Stanford, CA: Stanford University Press, 1957), 55: "That, then, is the ugly, broad ditch which I cannot

get across." Cf. Barth, *Theology of the Reformed Confessions*, 64: "Lessing's ugly ditch between eternal and rational truth and contingent historical truth had to open up."

182. German: *diesseits* ("here-and-now"); *jenseits* ("beyond").

183. German: *Aufhebung*, translated here and elsewhere as "sublation." See n. 63 above.

184. German: *der Geringste, der Schuldingste unter den Heiligen*. Here Barth uses both a play on words and a biblical allusion that cannot be rendered in English. With the first word, Barth alludes to 1 Cor. 15:9: "I am the least of the apostles" (*den geringsten unter den Aposteln*). The second word, *Schuldingste*, means the most guilty or greatest sinner. Thus, in Barth's paraphrase, Paul is "the *least*" (of the apostles) and "the *most* guilty" among the believers.

185. Friedrich von Schiller, *Die Braut von Messina oder Die feindlichen Brüder*, 4. Akt, 7. Szene.

186. Cf. Ps. 121:1. The translation attempts to convey Barth's rhetorical device of merging his sentences into the psalm. Cf. Barth, *Witness to the Word*, 2, where he employs the same verse and imagery to describe the work of biblical interpretation, paraphrasing Augustine.

187. "Christian life."

188. "Theology for pilgrims."

189. Cf. Mark 14:38; Luke 21:36.

# INDEX